I0458855

Healing TIME

MOVE INTO A FUTURE OF FREEDOM & FLOW

You will simply NEVER see the concept of "time" the same after reading this book. Once it clicks, there's no going back to believing your lack of progress is a "time management" problem. You'll unlock a new kind of presence, purpose, and momentum you didn't know was possible.

— **DR. FRANK BENEDETTO, PT,** *Founder of The HoneyBadger Project: A Healthcare Business Incubator*

Rebecca Hogg's *Healing TIME* is a powerful, compassionate guide for anyone feeling stuck between who they are and who they want to become. As a fellow therapist and someone who's had the joy of sharing the stage with Rebecca, I can say her warmth, insight, and wisdom shine through every page. She weaves together clinical experience, personal growth, and deep curiosity about time and healing in a way that's both accessible and transformative. This book isn't just theory — it's a gentle companion for anyone ready to reclaim their life, step by step, moment by moment. I'm so proud of her work.

— **ANDREA KYPRIANOU BAUM, MEd, LPC,** *Cofounder & Improv for Life Director at Stomping Ground Comedy Theatre & Training Center*

Rebecca has written the kind of book that meets you where you are — and gently walks you toward where you're meant to be. *Healing TIME* is a compassionate companion for anyone navigating anxiety, grief, or trauma, especially if therapy feels out of reach. Through her personal wisdom and the Healing TIME method, Rebecca reminds us that healing doesn't happen in time — it happens with it.

— **WES WOODSON,** *CEO of The Wes Woodson Company and Mental Health Speaker*

Healing TIME is that rare book that's grounded in the science of change, yet deeply human. Rebecca doesn't just offer a method, she offers perspective, structure, and language that actually shift how you think.

This book will help you step outside yourself and view your timeline, and the trajectories you might just make happen, if you take the right steps. Too often, we see neuroscience being overhyped. Here, she approaches impactful concepts with wisdom and clarity, in a way I believe many will resonate with.

— **DR. JUSTIN NICHOLS, PhD,** *Founder & CEO of Zencora | Inventor of Emotional Coherence™ and the Therapist Toolkit™ | Expert in Brain-Body Connections, Stress, and Neuroplasticity*

MOVE INTO A FUTURE OF FREEDOM & FLOW

Rebecca D. Hogg, LPC

Niche Pressworks
Indianapolis, IN

Healing TIME

Copyright © 2025 by Rebecca D. Hogg

All rights reserved. No part of this book may be used or reproduced in any manner whatsoever without prior written consent of the author, except as provided by the United States of America copyright law.

Most names, details, and identifying characteristics of individuals mentioned in the book have been changed to protect their privacy.

Scripture quotations marked (NIV) are taken from the Holy Bible, New International Version®, NIV®. Copyright © 1973, 1978, 1984, 2011 by Biblica, Inc.™ Used by permission of Zondervan. All rights reserved worldwide. www.zondervan.com The "NIV" and "New International Version" are trademarks registered in the United States Patent and Trademark Office by Biblica, Inc.™

For permission to reprint portions of this content or for bulk purchases, contact healingtime@canvascw.com

Author Photograph by Jeff Weadock
Published by Niche Pressworks; NichePressworks.com
Indianapolis, IN

ISBN
Hardcover: 978-1-962956-77-2
Paperback: 978-1-962956-76-5
eBook: 978-1-962956-75-8

Library of Congress Cataloging-in-Publication Data on File at lccn.loc.gov

The views expressed herein are solely those of the author and do not necessarily reflect the views of the publisher.

For More Resources...

As a small "Thank You" for purchasing my book, I'd like to give you some additional tools for *Healing TIME!*

YOU'LL RECEIVE:

- **VALUES CLARIFICATION** worksheet
- "If Time Were a Person..." **JOURNAL PROMPTS**
- Common **CORE BELIEFS** (see if yours are on it!)
- **SOMATIC EMBODIMENT PRACTICES**
- And **MORE!**

THEY'RE ALL AVAILABLE HERE!

https://canvascw.com/book/downloads

To the Creator, our Source, God:
You made our concept of Time, each of us, and
the rest of Creation, including what we have yet to discover.
Without You, nothing else would be possible.

To my parents who modeled courage, curiosity,
and compassion in learning and living what they
believed even in the face of rejection and judgment.

And to you, the reader:
Always remember you have powerful help co-creating your
life; you are not alone. May you continue to move forward
in your journey toward wholeness, remembering no matter
what comes along that may attempt to get you off your
path, the life you actually want can come from it.

Table of Contents

CHAPTER 1

Haunted by the Past

There is only one you for all time.
Fearlessly be yourself.

— ANTHONY RAPP

THE MOVIE THAT WOULDN'T STOP PLAYING

I lay awake, the normal, quiet 2:00 a.m. sounds of the house happening around me. I was exhausted, but the movie reel in my head wouldn't let me sleep.

Like a hateful demon, my mind forced me to watch the same scenes on a loop — again and again. I just wanted to sleep. I didn't want to think.

It didn't care.

Tonight's movie reel has two parts. Part one was inspired by a conversation I'd had earlier in the week, and part two was inspired by something from earlier today.

Part One: Sunday on Repeat

Earlier in the week, I had been at church, helping the rest of the women clean up the kitchen and the gathering room after a youth group meeting. My husband and I were very involved with the church. We were a team. Today was no different, though lately, I had been feeling disconnected. I was going through the motions, doing my duty as I saw it, but with an empty, restless feeling that seemed to be getting more pronounced.

One of the women, we'll call her Sally, had just had a major procedure, and it was her first day back after being out for a few weeks. I hadn't had a chance to talk to her until we were both standing near the sink. She was loading some serving utensils into the dishwasher while I wiped down the counter.

"How are you doing?" Sally asked as she rinsed frosting off the cake server.

"Pretty good," I replied, trying to make my voice neutral. "How about you?"

"Oh, I can't complain," she said. "How is your husband? I didn't get a chance to talk to him today."

I hoped my smile was convincing as I replied, "He's fine." I guessed he was. It was hard to tell; we didn't talk much these days. We'd even driven here separately. He'd been at the gathering, but he had to attend a meeting for the staff afterward, and it would be hours before he got home.

I couldn't tell her any of those things, of course. Those were things you didn't talk about with people you barely knew. Especially when you didn't want to see that look — the one where they're sympathetic and understanding, but underneath, you feel you're being judged as not good enough.

Because that was how the expectations felt. The message seemed to be that certain things in the marriage were the wife's responsibility to fix... and as the wife, if you couldn't, you were resigned to suffering the mess you had made for yourself. You couldn't blame your husband for those things; his actions were your fault, too. It wouldn't be that way if you were a better wife.

Those were the covert, if not overt, messages of marriage from religious institutions and others throughout my life that had firmly embedded themselves in my mind. It was up to me to keep things together and running smoothly.

I quickly turned the subject to something safer. "How are you feeling after your procedure?" And I thanked God when the conversation, like a perfectly orchestrated script, turned to doctors and pain meds, and my problems faded into the background. By the time she'd told me her whole story, I had finished wiping up the last of the scattered crumbs, wrung out the washcloth, and hung it on a peg to dry. Now, it was my opening to leave.

Even though I enjoyed my time with her, my goodbyes were, unfortunately, the most authentically cheerful thing I'd said all day as I made a beeline for the door. Finally, I could escape. These days, I didn't want to be around people. I was always evading the potential land mines of conversation topics that caused me to feel like I was a shell of myself. They were never the conversations I really needed.

As I walked out into the early afternoon sun and got into my car, I rejoiced in my felt sense of freedom, but only for a moment. Something kept bothering me. As I drove, I tried to figure out what it was.

It had been the exact kind of day I'd had hundreds of times before with the exact kind of conversation I had all the time.

The difference was that today, I had paid attention to it — not just the words, but everything underneath them.

The feeling of tension. The need to guard and pivot. The careful smile and the same deliberate, mild neutrality when I couldn't manage even the appearance of happiness.

The same feelings. The same worries. The same anxiety. The same relief when I could leave.

And today, the reason I wanted to leave was clear. What I really needed, which I knew from the counseling sessions I'd already been through, were real conversations, ones that held the authenticity of being seen and understood for who I really was and the pain of my experiences.

Something my therapist had asked me suddenly flashed into my mind.

"Where do you see your life in five years?"

The question had stunned me. I didn't know how to respond. It wasn't that I couldn't see what the future would be. The problem was that the future looked just like the present. And the present wasn't what I wanted.

The future I wanted didn't feel *possible*. I didn't seem to know how to make it happen. It seemed to depend on what others did or thought or on an elusive happiness I couldn't conjure up.

It wasn't just that way with my marriage; it was the same with other things I wanted, too. They never seemed to come to fruition. And these weren't over-the-top things like climbing Mount Everest, either. I just wanted simple things, like going home and taking a leisurely walk with my dogs or meeting up with friends for dinner or having a game night where I could simply smile and laugh because I was genuinely at ease and having fun.

I longed for authentic happiness and did not want to settle for a facade. I wanted to feel comfortable in my own skin again. I wanted to feel free.

Instead, I felt trapped. Why? Could I ever feel free again?

Even helping at the church didn't seem like something I would choose anymore. Everyone just seemed to assume that's what I would do, what I "should" do.

And yet... what did I want? Who was Rebecca under all the "shoulds?" What was Rebecca's future? Not the future she seemed destined to have, but the future she *wanted*?

As I pulled into the driveway, my mind ticked through the thoughts I always had.

Yes, I realize my marriage isn't great. Yes, some of that is my responsibility. And I'm working on it. We are trying therapy. What else can we do? I'm trying. What more do you want of me? What else can I do?

I wasn't sure who I was voicing all of that to. The world? Myself? God? No one in particular?

This internal conversation was something that happened a lot. And the answer to this question was always the same.

You need to do something different.

Something different. The thought just made me angry. *I've tried everything. What else can I try?*

Previously, there hadn't been an answer to that. Today, an answer came.

You can leave.

The response that flashed into my mind was instant and firm. *No! I cannot leave. Divorce is not an option.*

I got out of the car and fled into the house, leaving that mental conversation behind. Or so I wished.

Part Two: The Same Non-Argument

That was Sunday. Part two was a repeat of today's conversation with my husband.

It was another one of our same conversations. In this case, he told me his plans for while he was out of town; while I suspected some things weren't fully accurate, I accepted them to avoid looking angry or paranoid.

Whether or not the plans for going out of town were true, or how true they were, didn't even really matter now. The main problem was that there was nothing I could do either way.

I couldn't control his choices and felt like I couldn't control mine, either. I had been strongly encouraged at barely twenty years old to include the words, "I will never divorce you" in my wedding vows, and I naïvely did so because I had no plans to seek a divorce. Who on earth would think divorce is a possibility when planning their wedding? Unfortunately, those words became a trap.

If I chose to legally end my marriage when I had said I would never divorce him, would that make those words a lie? What would that say about me? What would the people I cared about think of me? Would I be a horrible person? And a failure? No matter how much pain I felt, I couldn't get past that thought process.

And that was always the reason. The commitment from the past weighed in my heart, too heavy to move. Back then, I wasn't strong enough to realize there were other options.

I would say to myself all the time, "Why is this happening? Why me?" I was doing all the "right" things, but they weren't working. Eventually, I realized it had never occurred to me to try to *truly understand* the situation from the perspective of someone who had more options than just staying in the marriage. I was thinking as if I were powerless instead of realizing I had choices.

A Revelation

Tonight, lying in bed after the frustrating conversation with my husband, something was different. Instead of hating the movie reel in my head, I suddenly realized that maybe it was trying to show me something.

I was a different person than the young girl who'd sworn that vow long ago. I had lived different experiences and gained different understandings about our relationship and about God as well.

At this point, I had been in therapy for more than seven years, with the main goal being to work on our marriage. I was making progress — if not on our marriage, on myself.

As I lay there, I thought of that question again — the one my therapist had asked me early on. "Where do you see your life in five years?"

Though I hadn't been able to answer then, it had started me thinking.

I suddenly sat up, remembering my notebook. One of my therapist's suggestions had been to write about how my relationship had impacted different facets of my life — the financial, existential, spiritual, relational, sexual, physical, emotional, mental, and other aspects. I got out of bed and turned on the light, smiling in spite of myself. He wasn't there, so I wasn't disturbing him even if it was now two-something a.m. on a Thursday.

I pulled the notebook out of the tote I carried it in and started looking at each part of my life. I realized that what was happening in those areas was not what I wanted or valued. I started writing feverishly, describing the current state of each of those categories. Maybe if I put it all on paper and out of my head, I could finally go to sleep.

As I wrote, I felt a heavy weight leaving my body, flowing into the words on the page.

When I looked at what I'd written, I felt a sense of amazement.

I saw with clarity how the areas of life I valued most were being devastatingly impacted by myself and others — particularly by the marriage relationship that had been a struggle at this point for over twelve years. The life I was living was completely different from the life I wanted and needed.

Surprised and dismayed, I set down my pen. So many things I valued were not very present in my life.

And ultimately, I was the one allowing it. The messages throughout my life were that if I did things a certain way in relation to dating and marriage, then marriage would be good overall, even though we'd have some normal marriage struggles. That obviously wasn't true, and yet the messages had set up those expectations.

"No more of this!" I thought firmly as I closed the notebook. It was time to set different boundaries to protect myself, heal myself, and give myself freedom to choose a different future.

It was time to draw a line in the sand.

"Those who sow with tears will reap with shouts of joy." (Psalm 126:5, NIV)

A NEW FUTURE BEGINS

The "line" was imaginary, but it was important. It was a boundary that divided time into the past and the future.

On one side was Past Rebecca, who had tried to act with good intentions when making choices and did her best at the time to follow through on them. On the other side was Future Rebecca, who saw that no matter what choices Past Rebecca had made, she needed to do things differently. Future Rebecca wanted to make choices that aligned with her values. She didn't want to live Past Rebecca's life because it would negatively impact her health and well-being.

In that moment, everything changed. I heard the two Rebeccas in my head and knew I was ready to change. The certainty felt as if it came from beyond myself — as if God and Future Me were somehow caring for Past Me and now Present Me.

The Line Between Past and Future

A good friend reminded me: "The best time to plant a tree is twenty years ago. The second-best time is now." That day was the day I planted a seed. I didn't wait for perfect conditions. I just decided — the best time is now.

At that moment, I stopped allowing Past Me to influence my present without any boundaries, and I gained a new understanding of Time that transformed how I chose to live.

When Past Me was in charge, I felt trapped in a cycle. I aimed for perfection in all things and relied on old ways of thinking to solve new situations. Neither set me up for success.

Instead, I constantly believed I wasn't good enough. I felt worn down and tired. I could never seem to find any peace or hope, yet I clung to these patterns out of fear. The misguided ideals, grief of past experiences, traumas, and beliefs haunted me through every decision.

Then I drew a line.

I created a boundary between Past Me and Future Me, and the line was there in the present. Present Me chose a different future. Staying in the same old pain and using the same coping methods were no longer options. Now, I would pursue healing by focusing on the values I wrote in my notebook and a commitment to change my situation. Every moment now became a valuable part of my healing journey.

This can happen for you, too. The tree you plant today can start growing *today*. Why wait? Every day you wait is a day of lost growth.

ELEMENTS OF HEALING

Healing takes time, in several forms. I've found this process involves three time-related elements:

- **Start a new era.** By drawing a line in the sand between the past and the future, you've set an intention for a new era — and this new era is intended as a time of healing.

- **Create time to heal.** To move forward, you need to set aside intentional moments devoted to *you* and meant specifically for healing.

- **Heal the aspects of Time within ourselves.** Past trauma and injuries and related grief and other emotions don't simply go away. These, as well as the associated beliefs and assumptions, need to be challenged and changed. Our past needs to be healed before we can move toward a healthier future.

"When we deny our stories, they define us.
When we own our stories, we get to write
a brave new ending." — BRENE BROWN[1]

WHAT IS TIME?

As you may have noticed, I'm fascinated by the concept of time. I enjoy films about time travel and alternative timelines, and that sense of curiosity influenced me as I thought about creating a therapeutic coaching program for people like me who wanted to get unstuck from overwhelming or unfulfilling situations. The secret, I realized, involved learning to see time differently.

Many of us think of time as a way to structure the day and schedule our lives: time to get up, time to go to work, or time to get the kids to school. In this way, it organizes our lives. For this book, we're going to think about time differently, seeing it as much more than a planning or scheduling tool. This bigger understanding of time will help you set the stage for healing.

Let's begin by defining time. It isn't just a way to organize your day. Time includes the past, present, and future, all of which are connected. My approach to healing recognizes how these moments in time are interconnected. They coexist and shape your experiences. What happened in the past influences how you respond in the present and can even shape your future self.

For me personally, I also see time as a mysterious power that's an aspect of God's nature, though, of course, nothing can fully describe this. Time invites us to grow and remember that we exist outside our everyday parameters. It involves different ways of approaching our lives. Regardless of your beliefs in a higher power, the concepts in this book work because of the way you'll recognize Time as a companion throughout your journey — past, present, and the you that's yet to come.

With intention and structure, Healing TIME will help you begin to untangle these moments so you can open the door to transformation. Think about it: You can heal the past while in the present, and those actions can directly and indirectly change the path of your life. Even the smallest actions today can deeply impact your future.

Healing TIME: The Basis of the Method

Deciding that you want a change prepares you to take the many small steps that will follow. I've organized the Healing TIME approach into four steps that will help you repair and redefine your relationship with time so that you can start living the healthy, fulfilling life you want.

Even the smallest actions today can deeply impact your future.

Each of these steps moves you through the healing process:

- Talk: Through Healing Talk, you'll begin to learn how to express your true feelings and thoughts. This will help you open yourself to new possibilities and achieve growth and healing.
- Investigation: Healing Investigation involves assessing important aspects of yourself and your situation, creating a plan to move forward, and preparing yourself for that movement.
- Movement: With Healing Movement, you take your first small steps — challenging yourself to build a better mental template, re-evaluating your progress, and unifying your body, mind, and spirit to work together for your good, not against you.
- Embodiment: Healing Embodiment begins when you start living as the new you, giving yourself grace to live positively while sharing with others in ways that give you abundant energy.

T alk
Connect, Communicate, Validate

I nvestigation
Assess, Plan, Prepare

M ovement
Step, Challenge, Reevaluate, Unify

E mbodiment
Live, Give Grace, Share

YOU CAN BREAK FREE

If you feel stuck in a toxic or stagnant cycle, unable to figure out what to do to get where you want to be, trust me, I understand. If you've tried things and they haven't worked, if you feel frustrated and despairing, I am here for you.

Healing TIME can help. It gives you the core practices of the therapeutic coaching method I've designed. It will help you break free so you can heal the past, embrace the present, and move confidently into the future.

As we go through, you'll learn the following:

- More about why you're missing opportunities and staying stuck.
- The four steps of the Healing TIME method.
- The secret power of the method and why it works.
- Some common setbacks and how to avoid them.

Each chapter includes actionable steps as well as exercises and reflections that help you work through ideas on a personal level to address what's going on and identify where you may need additional help — including therapy from a licensed professional or additional therapeutic coaching. Many of the tools in here (goal setting, affirmations, visualization, celebrating) are helping to retrain your brain's Reticular Activating System (RAS), which has been said to be your brain's superhero.[2]

Healing TIME was designed with a view of Time as less of a concept from which to schedule events. It is created in the understanding that Time is an integral piece of who you are, including the past, present, and future. It teaches you to understand your relationship with Time in a different way and encourages you to let that relationship heal you. It's about giving yourself permission to let go of what isn't serving you so you can live your life from a more (w)holistic or wellness-oriented perspective.

Throughout the book, you'll learn to create your own plan and watch it evolve as you learn and grow. And you just might surprise yourself. I want that surprise for you, too — more than you know!

With your dreams in mind, let's declare that your new era of healing begins right now so you can start working on a new you. This is your line in the sand; it's the beginning of your Healing TIME. Are you ready?!

VALUES EXERCISE: WHAT DO YOU REALLY WANT?

Let's begin with a quick exercise to get you thinking about what you truly want. I suggest getting your own notebook where you can keep your writings in one place, but you can just use loose-leaf paper if you prefer.

Make a page for each of the following major categories and list what you value and want within each.

1. Physical Well-being
2. Emotional Well-being
3. Mental Well-being
4. Relationships (social/family/friends, etc.)
5. Occupation/Career
6. Finances
7. Spirituality
8. Sexuality
9. Personal Growth
10. Quality of Life

For instance, in Physical Well-being, you could decide you want to be more physically fit so you can do more of the activities you enjoy. Or you could decide you want to tackle a chronic health issue. For Emotional Well-being, maybe you want to have more confidence and less fear during stressful situations. This is totally up to you. You don't have to stick only to these categories; add others if you want. Write down things you want even if you can't figure out what category they would belong in.

Now, after writing down your thoughts, take a look at each area. Are there any places where you feel you're struggling? Which areas might need healing? Where are you not feeling fulfilled or not expressing your true self? Where are the *shoulds* forcing you to be? Are there any strengths that can be leveraged from one category to another? It's amazing how everything is intertwined. Keep this notebook close. We'll refer back to it as we move along.

CHAPTER 2

The Opportunity You've Been Missing

Mindfulness gives you time.
Time gives you choices.
Choices, skillfully made, lead to freedom.
— HENEPOLA GUNARATANA

DIFFERENT CHOICES, NEW OUTCOMES

I can't say things magically got easier after that night when I realized some of the things I had been missing. My journey after that still had many difficult twists and turns. Those challenges never end because that's how life works. Yet, as you learn to make different choices, you discover you get different results.

Divorce terrified me for many reasons, including the fact that I had never lived alone. I had to navigate many fears, and living alone was just one, along with the "what ifs," like "What if I'll be alone for the rest of my life?"

However, as I learned to value each moment and listen for the opportunities to heal within it, I responded differently. And I learned to ask different questions.

Many faiths, perhaps inadvertently, often put the institution of marriage on a pedestal, and yet, I finally stopped asking, "How would people in church say God views divorce?" Instead, I asked, "How does God view *me*? And would the way He views me change EVEN IF I got divorced?"

That answer was very different and full of peace. God could see my heart. He knew not only Past Rebecca but also Current and Future Rebecca. He knew everything about me, including why I made the decisions I did. I didn't have to explain or get permission from a human. It was between Him and me.

I realized my husband and I were on very different pages of very different books. Just like me, he was another real, flawed person, and our problems were enough to warrant divorce. I didn't *want* to be divorced. However, I also needed to honor and show care for all of me — just as I was also taught by that same religious institution. It was time to move on.

I reached out to others I could trust and found what I needed — from a listening ear to a compassionate heart to tough questions asked in concern for my best interest. I also knew some of the people I loved would staunchly disagree with my decisions and even stand in judgment of them rather than seeking to understand, comfort, or empathize with me. I battled that loneliness and fear, along with the frustration of others' well-meaning advice that put the burden back on me again.

As I asked different questions and made different choices, I began to embody what I learned in therapy and in my personal journey with myself and God. My fear of being alone faded as I realized it was just another type of experience I needed to see differently and find happiness in, which I began to do as I learned to enjoy time alone.

During this time, I also had many unique and fun experiences while doing new things to heal and grow. I decided to try things like dancing, acting, and improv to get out of my comfort zone and learn to think more on my feet. To generate more income, I decided to rent out some rooms in my house and ended up making friends with one of my renters, a Swedish woman whom I've since traveled to visit in Sweden a couple of times. Then someone from Turkey rented a room. We also became friends, and I visited her as well. I also started doing public speaking — something I initially feared. I learned and experienced new healing modalities, and of course, I wrote this book! These were only some of the unexpected gifts along the way, many of which came out of what had been my deepest pain.

As I gained new friends, internal strength, and shifts in perspective, I finally started to feel more and more of what I'd wanted to feel: peace, joy, and curiosity for life!

They were there, hidden in each moment. I just had to look for and find them as I discovered new parts of myself.

WHY WE GET STUCK

The key to getting unstuck is understanding how and why we get stuck in the first place. When we are struggling in this way, we often feel like we've tried so many things, and nothing works. It gets *very* frustrating! We can sink into despair, feeling there's simply no solution for our particular situation.

I never want anyone to feel this way — including you.

The truth is that there are many possible solutions. When we haven't yet found them, it might be because we shy away from making the changes they require. Instead of facing the painful or uncomfortable thing, we try lots of things we're comfortable with, and maybe even some we're *less* uncomfortable with. And we end up staying in our stuck place. We tell ourselves, "Things are fine as they are." We continue coping as best we can. And honestly, as a therapist, I truly understand that sometimes that's the best we can do right then. Trying to face something when we're not ready can sometimes be damaging as well.

However, those coping solutions are only temporarily helpful. If extended for too long, they bring their own price. Though things seem *fine*, underneath, we're expending energy toward "not rocking the boat" instead of toward something we need.

Over time, we can start to feel overwhelmed in one way and unfulfilled in another. There's a saying that "*fine*" can often stand for "Feelings Inside, Not Expressed." The negative vibrational energy of those unexpressed feelings can build up and either implode (creating physical health issues) or explode (impacting relationships with others and our life situations). Neither of these outcomes is desirable.

"Fine" can often stand for "Feelings Inside, Not Expressed."

Resisting change basically amounts to staying under the influence of the past, whether we want to or not, or whether we even realize it. Let's look at some of the reasons we may resist change so we can begin to untangle them and move forward.

F eelings

I nside

N ot

E xpressed

FIVE REASONS YOU COULD BE STRUGGLING WITH CHANGE

All of the following common reasons we struggle with change involve the dynamic of time, even if it's not obvious at first. Figuring out what's going on is a little like a treasure hunt. And once you identify and can see the problem, you are no longer allowing it to hold the same power over you; you can begin creating new opportunities for healing.

1. Childhood Events Have Left a Mark

Development starts *in utero* and is particularly important during the formative years from birth up to eight years old.[3] Some things in childhood that affect us are overt, meaning they're clear and have had an obvious effect. However, some are more covert, meaning they are under the surface and affect our thoughts without our realizing it. Our caregivers' treatment of us, our family relationships, stressful events such as poverty or homelessness... all these and more can leave lasting marks on us. The CDC published an overview of findings from several studies regarding adverse childhood experiences, or ACEs.[4] The article lists examples of "potentially traumatic events" that occur in childhood, defined as the years between birth to seventeen, including violence, abuse, neglect, substance abuse by household members, and others. Due to these traumas and their accompanying grief, we often carry coping beliefs and behaviors well into adulthood, resulting in chronic disease, injury, and even limited life opportunities.

The good news is that they can be mitigated through therapy and other self-work. The key is to give yourself the opportunity to heal — you need Healing TIME.

2. Unproductive Beliefs Create Negative Cycles

What beliefs have we adopted from things in our past? Oftentimes, we don't even realize how these beliefs could be filtering our thoughts in a way that creates a negative cycle in our lives. Dr. Peter Grinspoon explains how these "cognitive distortions" can take many forms.[5]

He describes things like black-and-white or all-or-nothing thinking, the idea we *should* or *must* be doing something, or the habit of labeling ourselves, among many others. These beliefs aren't based on facts but often come from experiences. Left unchallenged, they can create far more anxiety in our lives than is needed. These anxieties will, in turn, create more resistance to change than we would normally have. This is why it's important to set aside time to challenge the core beliefs that aren't helping you.

3. We Fear Giving Up Control to the Unknown

Take a piece of paper (or, better yet, pull out that notebook!) and draw a vertical line down the middle of a page, making two columns. On the top left, write "Can Control," and on the top right, write "Cannot Control." Now, list the things that are bothering you and put them in the appropriate column. Are they world events? Other people's opinions and thoughts? What is taking your mental energy? Write them in the appropriate column. Be one hundred percent honest with yourself about what you can control versus what you cannot.

Imagine holding sand in the palm of your hand. If you were to grip it tightly, it would begin to seep out from every direction, and the tighter you grasped it, the more sand you would lose, and whatever is left starts to hurt your hand. However, if you released your grip into a cupped position and just let the sand sit in your hand, it would remain in place and stay within your palm.

The harder you try to grasp things that are out of your control, the less control you will actually have over those things. Continuing this impossible attempt will leave you in a state of anxiety, pain, depression, or feeling lost or powerless. You will not want to change when you're in those mental states. And yet, if you could surrender control, wouldn't you want it to be under the power of a higher, all-seeing influence? This is one of the ways Healing TIME will help you: by helping you trust what you can't yet see.

4. Past Experiences Teach Us We Are Powerless

A sense of powerlessness comes from a lack of belief or confidence in ourselves. The need to control things, as mentioned in point three, and our failure to do so is one reason we can feel powerless. Past experiences, messages we received growing up, traumatic relationships, and/or grief experiences can all reshape our ability to navigate our inner systems in a healthy way. As a result, they can leave us with damaged confidence in ourselves.

Feeling powerless does *not* have to be a permanent state. It is possible to change this belief and gain greater agency or self-empowerment. If we can shift focus to what we *do* have autonomy over (our internal systems: thoughts, feelings, emotions, etc.), we can eventually break free from the prison of self-doubt and panic.

Healing TIME allows us to create small wins, shifting our thoughts from the negative and unhelpful to the positive and helpful, thereby relieving the suffering, regardless of our circumstances. I am not saying this is always easy. I am not dismissing the difficulty and distress of life. However, I know people can heal from the most tragic of situations. Holocaust survivor Viktor Frankl, who went on to do incredible work in psychiatry, psychology, and philosophy, is a prime example. We may still have pain, grief, uncomfortable experiences, and trauma, but the goal is not to allow those things to take over our inner selves. We deserve to have agency over our lives. We can be happy and still function, even while experiencing grief, sadness, and other painful and unpleasant emotions.

5. *Our Identities Are Based on Our Status Quo*

Oftentimes, we're too focused on trying to please others. Our behavior is determined by what we *should* do or what we've always done because that's what we believe others want. Consequently, we will naturally resist things that take us out of that familiar identity.

If we label ourselves as "reliable" and we see change as making us "unreliable," then we won't want to change. We want to keep the good image we've created in our minds. When that image doesn't fully reflect or allow our whole person to be present, we suffer and feel unfulfilled.

Who are you as a person? Can you answer that about yourself? It's a broad question but also important. Many of my clients come to me because they can't answer it. They've been so focused on being that desired image of themselves, they have forgotten how to think about who they really are and what they really want. Healing TIME gives you opportunities to discover those answers in each new moment.

THERE'S A BETTER WAY

I allowed myself to suffer for many years. The reason I eventually could understand what was happening was not because I made "just the right change at the right time." It was actually the complete opposite.

I made a lot of small changes that eventually took me to different places in my timeline, even though I didn't know where exactly I would be going.

That's the secret — or at least part of it. When you get used to challenging yourself with the small things, dealing with the huge ones doesn't seem so overwhelming.

When you get used to challenging yourself with the small things, dealing with the huge ones doesn't seem so overwhelming.

I had been challenging myself with more physical exercise, doing therapy, and many other new things. As I built confidence from these, I eventually felt emotionally able to address new challenges — the ones I hadn't been seeing as clearly. The ones I was just coping with.

If I hadn't started with the first tiny step, the rest may never have happened, and I would not be writing this book that you are now reading.

It was a process, however. It started with how I saw myself within the framework of my relationship with Time, and the more I understood how I was working with Time (and how it was working with me), the more I was able to use it in a positive way to transform my life. Time is full of opportunities. The way we approach each moment determines not just whether we make the most of them but whether we even notice them at all.

Two Kinds of Time: Make the Most of Them

Did you know that the ancient Greeks had two different words for time? The first, "Chronos," means measurable/sequential time, which can be quantified — days, hours, minutes, and so on. The second word, "Kairos," refers to the qualitative idea that certain moments are more or less important than others.[6]

26

Most of us at least understand the measurable aspect of time, as our civilization depends on synchronizing activities to get things done. We also generally understand the fact that our experience of time seems to change based on what we're doing — some parts of the same day can seem to fly by, while others seem to last much longer.

It's important to work within both aspects of time when approaching your daily activities. We can often feel like we should measure every minute and be super-efficient. Yet, as we do so, we can forget to savor the moments. We feel rushed and powerless, as if we "never have any time."

Conversely, we can also get so caught up in a single moment that we allow it to dominate us for days or weeks — even the rest of our lives. Do you ever look back at a choice you made that took only moments, yet you still regret it and carry that burden with you? Do you maybe even make up a future fear and look at it every so often?

To heal, we need to be aware of how we can productively use both of these concepts to work with us. We need to ensure we devote enough measurable time toward the results we want, and yet, we also need to value the experiences we have within the moments we are giving to them. Without both aspects of time, we become less effective and less able to achieve the goals we've set, including the goal of just enjoying and having peace in the moment. Don't we all want more of that? I know I certainly do!

If Time Were a Person: What's Your Relationship?

Let's expand on Chapter 1's idea of Time as a companion.

In therapy, whether as an individual, a couple, or a family, we consider the interplay of the dynamics of people. Each person is to be heard. So, let's consider how we are interacting with and responding to Time (Them).

Do you feel constantly rushed, never finished with anything, always trying to live up to the impossible standards *you believe* Time has set for you? Or does Time wait patiently — savoring the moment with you, enjoying the scenery, laughing with friends, doing the project you've been wanting to do, or whatever else you're interested in right then?

Imagine Time not as a resource or a harsh master but as a person, even a companion that we can interact with and have a relationship with. Have you asked Them to help you get where you really want to go? Do you believe in Their power to help take you there? Or are you just passively going along but then complaining when you're not getting what you want?

We talk a lot about Time, but do we stop to truly listen to and understand Them? Do you want Time to just say "yes" to you, or have you asked Them to reveal truth to you, even if it stings? Do you allow Them to help you heal and grow in order to become what you are capable of?

What do you blame on Time? What could you do instead that would be a healthy, ideal response? What would it look like to go with the flow, to essentially dance with Time? Do you constantly put Them down, saying They are never enough?

Do you feel Time is out to get you? Are you cowering with fear or avoiding Them? Or do you go through cycles where you embrace Time but then push Them away?

Let's allow ourselves to get to know and experience Time the way we experience the best relationships — through seeking to understand, taking responsibility, and finding peace, gratitude, and joy together.

TIMELINE EXERCISE: WHAT GOT YOU HERE?

How did you get to be the person you are today, reading this book now?

It's helpful to understand what got you here. To help my clients answer this question, I have them create a picture of their lives to organize important life events. Don't worry! You don't have to draw anything. Instead, you're going to create a timeline of your life.

Take out a piece of blank paper and turn it so it's in landscape mode, with the long side at the bottom. Now, draw a line across the middle from left to right. The left end of the line is the beginning/when you were born. The end of the line on the right is now, this moment.

Now, make some little marks along the line for every five or ten years. It doesn't have to be perfect; you just need to be able to see where things generally occurred.

Figure 2.1 Timeline Example

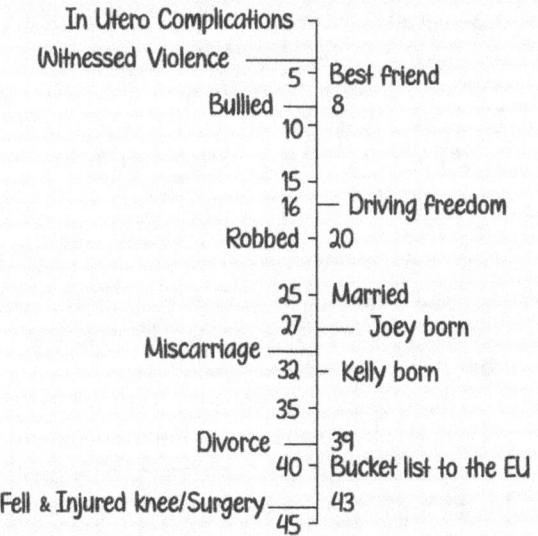

(The example shown is shown vertically to be able to fit within the size of this book. For your purposes, you'll be drawing yours horizontally.)

Within each five- or ten-year segment, start noting important things that happened to you or that you achieved in your life. If you feel something was positive or even neutral, write it above the line around where it happened. If it was a traumatic or negatively impactful event that caused grief, write it below. If there was a period of time when something was positive/pleasant or negative/unpleasant, you could mark it appropriately to show the general trend for that time period. See the example in Figure 2.1.

If you feel it's going to take more than one sheet of paper to write everything so that you can read it, tape two sheets together on the back or get a longer sheet of paper.

When you've drawn this timeline and plotted all these events, take a moment to look at everything and consider the following questions.

1. If the timeline tells a story about you, what story does it tell? How does that story cause you to feel? What is the reason for this feeling?
2. Do you feel this timeline says all there is to say about you? Why or why not?
3. Is there a noticeable difference in the number of things above and below the line? If so, what meaning do you make of that?
4. How did the events below the line affect those above it and vice versa? Are some of the good/ pleasant things a byproduct of the bad/unpleasant things that happened?
5. Are there any events you wish were on the timeline but aren't? What are those events? What emotions do you feel (e.g., grief, sadness, bitterness, loss, emptiness) about those events that aren't there? Have you processed their absence?

Hold onto this timeline — we're going to use it later.

CHAPTER 3

Let Yourself Believe

Time is the wisest counselor of all.

— PERICLES

After I adopted a different perspective on my marriage, my life went through a whirlwind of change. I finally decided that divorce would be a healthy step forward for me rather than a failure. Though it was difficult, I chose to do it. Between therapy and other changes in my life, I had made so much personal progress that I felt at peace and relatively calm working through the situation despite its difficulty. And then, life threw me a curveball.

At that time, I was fairly content in my job as a counselor at a disciplinary alternative school, and I thought I could be there as long as I chose. I had what felt like security and a comfortable way to support my life.

Then, about six months after my divorce, I was told the school district had decided to eliminate some positions, including mine. At first, all I could think about was how it was not ideal timing. I was just trying to get used to being on my own. Financially, I had no other person to lean on while I looked for another job and was trying to build my savings back up. Panic started to set in. What would I do?

I started thinking. I had assumed I'd be a counselor in a school for life (like I had assumed I'd be in my marriage for life). Now, I had a chance to reevaluate that belief. I could take the same route, do the same thing — or I could do something new.

Something new. Hmmm.

I remembered a conversation a few months prior about starting and growing a successful private practice. At the time, I had dismissed it almost entirely as a pipe dream, but now, that thought wouldn't leave my mind.

It was a seemingly crazy idea, and I had plenty of reasons not to do it. I had just gone through a divorce. I had no nest egg, no cushion, no sense of security. And I needed benefits. I couldn't possibly go into private practice, could I?!

And so, I told myself that wasn't an option and applied for different school counselor positions.

And that's when it really started getting difficult. When I interviewed at a school, it felt weird, like it wasn't right for me. I realized that even if I took a job at a school, I would feel like I was dying inside. Now that things were shaken up, I got honest with myself. I didn't want to keep working at a school.

Don't get me wrong. Counseling in schools is a great profession, and counselors can really make a difference. Everyone's dream is different, and that might be someone's true calling. For me, it was a great experience, yet it wasn't my dream anymore, and it took having my position eliminated for me to realize that I could see what else was out there. I needed to move into something new — the next challenge where I could make a difference in a new way while also having more freedom in my schedule and time for other things I didn't even know I wanted yet.

I took some time to seriously consider it. I prayed and even fasted while trying to listen for what to do next. And the answer was clear enough. I needed to open my own private practice.

Future Me wanted me to follow this dream. Time was my guide in this decision. I know I would have regretted not choosing the seemingly scarier but more fulfilling path.

"Okay... here we go!" I thought to myself on the day I finally made the decision. I took the first steps and never looked back. At least, not yet!

Even a year before, I could not have imagined opening my own practice. My outlook and my confidence levels had changed so much that now I could see that it was possible, and I recognized the opportunity when it came. Previously, I may have seen the elimination of my position as a hardship or a setback. Now, instead of looking at it through those filters, I asked, "Okay, what kind of opportunity is this giving me?" And this way of thinking has been helpful ever since!

THE SECRET TO GETTING PAST THE UNKNOWN

One of the hardest parts of getting unstuck is when you don't want to stay where you are, but you're not sure how to get to something new. You feel like you don't have enough information.

This lack of information can stop you in your tracks.

When working with clients over the years, I have noticed they usually define their situation in one of two ways (though it can also be a mix of both).

In one situation, there's a nebulous goal, and the steps to attain it are a little unclear; or perhaps they know a few of the steps to take, but the rest seem fuzzy. In the other situation, the goal is clearer, but some steps to get there are completely missing.

In both of these instances, the secret is actually quite simple: You need to build the steps you don't have, and the <u>first step to doing that is building your belief in yourself.</u>

> You need to build the steps you don't have, and the first step to doing that is building your belief in yourself.

A Nebulous Goal and a Short Ladder

When you have an unclear goal, you know what you want in very general terms. For instance, you may want to "feel better" or "change your life." While you aren't sure exactly what "better" looks like, you know that something doesn't feel right. You may feel disconnected or as if something in general isn't working, but you're not sure exactly what.

Figure 3.1 A Nebulous Goal and a Short Ladder

It's like you're looking at a place up in the clouds, sort of hazy and far away. You can't quite reach that place, and yet something about it is calling to you. You just need a ladder to climb up there, but the ladder you have isn't long enough. It's a step ladder, and you need an extension ladder, like on a fire truck.

If only you could see more of that place to know if it's worth going there or even if it's possible. To do that, you would need to climb higher up on a taller ladder you don't have. So, you don't do anything, and therefore, you don't get anywhere. Nothing changes if nothing changes.

A Clear Goal and a Ladder with Missing Rungs

On the other hand, if you have a clear goal, you understand what you could have up there on the cloud. The problem is that your ladder, while long enough, is missing some rungs in the middle, and you don't see how to get there without those.

This is the situation my client Marie found herself in. Here's what she wrote about her own story:

It was early October, and I was up at 3:00 a.m., preparing for a tropical storm. The sweltering heat filled the air, so thick I could almost choke.

The ominous sky mirrored the way I felt. I was exhausted, in pain, and ready to give up.

For five years, I had been the sole caregiver for my aging parents, both in decline with dementia. Two car accidents had shattered my physical health, leaving me in chronic pain and unable to work. As I was recovering, my mom was diagnosed with cancer. The next several months were filled with testing, surgery, sickness, and six weeks of radiation treatments. Just afterward, my dad had major spinal reconstructive surgery and experienced complications that delayed his recovery.

Then Things Got Worse

The next thing I knew, I was sitting in the emergency room after a friend noticed I was slurring my speech and seemed disoriented. I told myself I had just overdone things and was stressed out. Unfortunately, it wasn't "just stress." It turned out I had Type 2 diabetes, along with other health issues I hadn't been listening to my body about.

This was the beginning of a journey through chronic illness — on top of the pain I already dealt with. I followed all the medical guidelines, but the medication wasn't working. To make things worse, my physician passed away four months into my treatment. He wasn't just my doctor; he was also a dear friend and a big part of my emotional support network.

I felt as if the ground had disappeared from under my feet, along with all my hope of getting better. With no medical insurance, no employment, and no prospects for continued medical care, I decided to ignore the issues and carry on with life, doing the best I could. Settling back into old ways and familiar vices to cope, I developed severe sleep apnea. I couldn't get my CPAP machine to work for me, and I woke up every night feeling like I was choking or drowning. The resulting sleep deprivation further undermined my health.

Surviving the Storm

That morning, as the storm faded, I surveyed the wreckage, feeling a strange sympathy for the broken trees and damaged buildings. My brain and body were in ruins. I was losing my sense of identity and even the will to live.

It's a strange feeling to feel thankful you made it through another night alive while at the same time dreading the thought of having to survive another day and wishing that you could just go to sleep forever.

Suddenly, I knew I had to do something different, or I wasn't going to make *it. What I had been doing wasn't enough. Something had to change. I had to face the storm head-on and figure out how to weather through.*

I realize now that morning was my own "line in the sand," as Rebecca says. It was the day I chose to have something different, though I had no idea how or what yet.

New Hope

Flash forward to January. As I sat in my bedroom one afternoon, vacillating between hopeless sobs and striving for renewed vision, I reached out to Rebecca, who would likely have some ideas for how I could start fighting to really live again.

She reminded me how important my life was and that the dismissive attitudes I met thus far in the medical world were unacceptable. She also reminded me that giving up wasn't a solution and that it was important to talk with trusted friends and to remind myself of my own value.

With this validation, a tiny spark of hope reappeared, and I started healing time.

Marie had a specific goal: She wanted to solve her health issues. Unfortunately, life seemed to be hitting her from all sides, and she felt overwhelmed not only by problems but also by the sense that her goal was impossible. Nothing she did seemed to bring helpful answers.

Do you relate to this? Have you tried things that didn't work and told yourself that your situation was hopeless? Are you getting through your day, and yet underneath, you're overwhelmed by despair and depression? Do you feel like life is trying to knock you off the ladder while you're trying to replace the missing rungs?

Figure 3.2 A Solid Goal and a Ladder with Missing Rungs

TAKE POWER: BUILD YOUR BELIEFS

We've probably all been in either of the ladder situations before. Though each is a little different, they both can keep us stuck in the "now." I don't mean in the healthy present moment type of now but rather in the suffering now. Unfortunately, the situations we're in often can cause us to feel it is impossible to see the steps that will get us to the future. We don't know what actions to take or, in the first instance, whether taking action is even worth the effort.

When your ladder is missing rungs, what it's missing are the beliefs and related actions to take you to the goal.

This is what the Healing TIME framework is based on: creating a belief in yourself through actions that can take you to your goal and subsequently feeling what you are looking for. It works because it keeps negative patterns from sabotaging you. We're helping you create new healthy and healing patterns.

When your ladder is missing rungs, what it's missing are the beliefs and related actions to take you to the goal.

When I started my journey, I didn't have a clear goal. I just wanted to feel better about my life, find peace, and feel comfortable in my own skin. These were more general goals. Yet working toward them required me to try many different new things. I challenged myself and got out of my comfort zone. These small changes developed a strong belief in myself, and this showed up when I decided to open my private practice. In the past, I would have clung to the seeming security of a familiar job.

Small changes build toward bigger changes, and small successes lead to bigger ones. Even if there's an occasional step back, this step-by-step process develops greater confidence and belief in yourself.

Marie knew and valued where she needed to go. She knew she valued her health, but until she clarified what that meant in terms of her thoughts and actions, she couldn't move forward. She didn't have the *belief* to create more ladder rungs of action steps that would get her there. Until she created those, she/Present Marie and Future Marie seemed divided by an impassible chasm of hopelessness.

Marie had to decide she would find the solution and focus on believing in that rather than in the hopelessness she was tempted to feel. When she started making decisions from Future Marie's perspective, she came from a place of belief in herself and her own healing with Time. Hopelessness didn't have any place to be when belief was present.

PUT YOUR BELIEF IN THE FUTURE

When you believe in the dream coming alive, almost anything is possible. Instead of scapegoating Time for keeping you from doing something, invest time in finding the solutions you need.

The first step, however, is to shift perspectives by choosing to believe a different story. Most of your beliefs have been coming from the past, which has taught you lessons like *you can't*, *they won't*, or *you don't know how*. These beliefs keep you paralyzed.

It's time to find a new source of belief, one that comes from a place of certainty. Doesn't it make sense for it to come from the place where what you're working toward already exists?

You guessed it: The future is that place. And Future You is that source.

The future is your guide in Healing TIME. With the belief of Future You, you will be able to make the progress you haven't before. You can start climbing up the ladder because you'll see how to build the missing rungs.

The future is your guide in Healing TIME.

When you imagine yourself in the future, who do you see? Social scientists at UCLA explored this question by studying the brain activity of people as they thought about their present selves, their future selves, and other people. They discovered something interesting. For most people, their future self feels like a stranger — someone they don't know.

Hal Hershfield, a social psychologist involved in the study, explained, "One of the reasons people fail to make good choices and don't act in ways that are positive in the long term is because they feel a sense of disconnect from their future selves."[7]

To bridge that gap, researchers used virtual reality technology to show participants older versions of themselves, as if they were looking into a mirror from the future. Across four different studies focused on financial decision-making, participants who had stronger connections to their future selves were more likely to make long-term, beneficial decisions rather than give in to short-term gratification.

Connecting with yourself in the future gives you much more power over your own thoughts, beliefs, and decisions. When you're friends with the version of Future You, who is already where you want to be, they can guide you. They aren't afraid of where you're going and how you get there because they are already there. With Future You as your ally, you can go practically anywhere. And if you're friends with Future You, you naturally want to do more for them now.

Are you ready to put Future You in charge of working with Time? You'll learn how in the next chapters. Until then, I ask you to believe that healing *is* possible for you. Even if you can't quite see how to get there, give yourself permission to have that tiny spark of hope. If it's difficult, borrow that belief from me until you make it your own. I'm excited to see what it can do for you!

CHAPTER 4

Healing TIME

We all have our time machines.
Some take us back; they're called memories.
Some take us forward; they're called dreams.

— JEREMY IRONS

The Healing TIME framework is effective because it helps create a belief in yourself that empowers you to take specific actions that can move you toward your goal. As Mel Robbins said in a social media post, "You are ONE decision away from a completely different life... A life you dream about. A life that is MEANT for you."[8] Every day, you have the opportunity to make that decision.

Because this approach is holistic, I want to start by briefly explaining each step of the Healing TIME process: Talk, Investigation, Movement, and Embodiment. This way, you'll be able to see how the individual steps work on their own and as a whole to support your transformation.

The Healing TIME framework is loosely based on the six stages of change, which include pre-contemplation, contemplation, preparation, action, maintenance, and relapse.[9] As you learn more about each element of Healing TIME, you'll see that they include foundational thought from those six stages. However, the Healing TIME framework differs in that it isn't necessarily a set of sequential steps. As you'll see, many of the steps can be happening in different ways at the same time. However, similar to the six stages model, the Healing TIME framework recognizes that change often happens in cycles.

Healing TIME also goes a step further by focusing on ways to help you break free from the beliefs and behaviors that keep you stuck. It provides specific tools and approaches that help you recognize and release your unproductive beliefs that are leading to equally unproductive behaviors and keeping you where you are. That's why an important part of this work is learning to relate to Time differently. When you see the past, present, and future in a new way, healing and breaking free become possible.

USING TIME TO GET UNSTUCK

Healing TIME is designed to help you use the dynamics of time to get unstuck. Instead of viewing time as simply a measurement tool to organize the day, you can learn to embrace it as a powerful way to relate to yourself. By seeing your past, present, and future selves, you learn how these different aspects of self can influence you.

Do you remember the values exercise you completed in Chapter 1? You identified what was important to you. I hope you've also started to think about how to get there.

Part of being able to live according to your values involves setting boundaries in your life. As you saw in my story, I had to draw a boundary between my past and future to keep my past beliefs from causing me to keep doing the same unproductive things. That's what this system will help you do. You will move toward your values and develop strategies to protect them from old habits.

You'll also learn to put boundaries around your thoughts and behaviors so that you don't spend time on negative, unproductive actions that don't support your values and goals.

Empowering ourselves to set boundaries helps us relate to time as a force of change in our lives, and we can start seeing more opportunities and make different choices than we've made in our past — even when the past is only yesterday.

Even when I was taking action, I would sometimes still end up moving backward. That finally shifted when I began living according to this model of time, and it's helped others, too. It also helps me see where clients have been stuck in a cycle so I can help them more quickly.

THE FOUR COMPONENTS OF HEALING TIME

Let's look at the four main elements of Healing TIME: Talk, Investigation, Movement, and Embodiment. When you think about these things, it makes more sense to put the word Healing in front of them. They become Healing Talk, Healing Investigation,

Healing Movement, and Healing Embodiment. Wow! Think about that for a moment: Within these two-word phrases, all of these aspects of time are rolled into healing you and keeping you healthy going forward. That is an incredible thought. How can you *not* succeed if Time itself is focused in all those ways for your own healing?

T alk

I nvestigation

M ovement

E mbodiment

(Healing) Talk

We talk all the time, but Healing Talk is different. It is about mindfully connecting for a mutual benefit toward healing.

We are made to connect with other people, animals, and even things. We need to be able to share ideas, thoughts, emotions, and experiences with someone we care about and who cares about us. Healing Talk is the first step toward that.

Healing Talk is also about connecting with ourselves. We can't forget that we are important in the connections we make, too.

Connection includes verbal interactions as well as writing, reading, and our own internal dialogue. Even writing in your notebook is a form of Healing Talk. For me, writing was a way of communicating with myself. It was this component that allowed me to process what was happening and also to feel validated. When I drew my "line in the sand," I didn't suddenly get there. My journaling, therapy, and other communications helped me arrive at that important moment.

Communication involves being vulnerable. It takes courage. This is why it is good to have a healthy support system. Along with my therapist, my close friends, colleagues, and others were there for me. And I learned to trust and allow myself to be vulnerable with them because I felt emotionally safe enough to do so.

(Healing) Investigation

The second letter, **I**, is for Investigation. To get where I wanted to go, I needed to take the time to look at where I had been and where I was currently. Time played a large role here. I investigated the differences between Past Me and Future Me. I devoted time to doing the investigation.

It was during the Investigation phase that I tried to understand what was happening — why did I feel the way I was feeling?

Because the Investigation phase involves questioning thoughts, habits, and feelings, it can be scary because it's unknown. Yet investigating these areas sheds light on them and can help us face the fear.

To reframe fear, you can think of it as **False Evidence Appearing Real**. By investigating and doing thoughtful research, you can separate truths from false evidence.

Fear is False
Evidence
Appearing
Real.

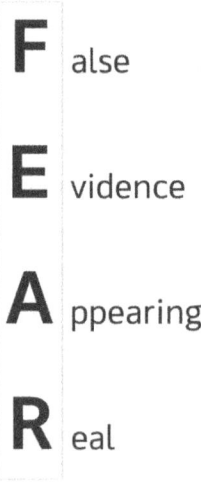

F alse

E vidence

A ppearing

R eal

Investigating helped me accomplish this through the exploration and clarification of my values. In this way, Investigation and Talk worked together. My writings were both self-talk and an investigation. I communicated my feelings as I wrote them down, and an investigative approach encouraged me to delve deeper and ask more questions. Both helped me define my path and my values. There wasn't a linear "this, then that" process.

Investigation reminded me to look more deeply into the moment I was in and where it fell on my journey. I started to understand how it related to the past, present, and future elements of my life. My beliefs in the current moment could affect how I saw the past and also how I saw and created the future. I started to realize that the future I was previously creating for myself wasn't the one I wanted. What I needed to know more about was how to have the future I wanted but hadn't yet experienced.

It's easy to think about investigating what has happened in the past or what's going on right now, but how do you investigate a future that hasn't happened yet?

This goes back to the nebulous goals we talked about earlier. Your future can be what you choose to make it — so wouldn't you want to build it around your values? What would it look like if you did that? Your goal needs to have multiple dimensions for you to know what it really is. You need to see it and be inside it as if you're walking around in virtual reality. If you can't visualize it, how can you make it real? How can you see the segments that don't make sense yet?

(Healing) Movement

Okay, I know this sounds like I'm talking about yoga or some other healthy exercise, but **M** is for the type of Movement that involves taking steps toward the change you want. It is the action of shifting your beliefs and expectations so they align with your values. It often focuses on making different choices.

The movement step could include physical movement if one of the things you're trying to do is get healthier. More commonly, however, it focuses on smaller shifts in your choices and habits.

At times, you may feel frustrated because you are doing different things, but nothing seems to be happening. It's important to remember that movement is shaking things up, even if they don't feel like they're changing right away. It's helpful to remember that every new action is making a change, even one you don't see yet.

Sometimes, the effect builds and then happens suddenly, all at once. After my line in the sand, I started changing things that did not seem connected to each other. Along with writing in my notebook, I walked more (at the gym and with a friend) and tried a lot of new things I had never done before. I also went to an integrative and functional medicine provider for a full blood work assessment.

I learned a great deal about myself and how my body functions. These things were all part of my process and how I discovered more about myself. At that time, I didn't see any direct relationship between these actions; it was all part of the energy in motion that makes up our emotions. Yet they all gave me more knowledge that took me forward and helped me make different decisions.

Movement in one area of life can also affect other areas. On that sleepless night I described in Chapter 1, I had already made just enough changes in my life to open my mind in different ways. Looking through my notebook and reading my notes about what I wanted from life, I compared them to what I actually had. Suddenly, I realized that nothing changes if nothing changes. BING! A light bulb went off. I realized that prior to that, I had formed some strong limiting beliefs. Movement of all kinds had already helped me break through some of those limits enough to see differently here, too. And, if I could change things in those other areas, couldn't I change things in this one?

This can happen for you, too.

(Healing) Embodiment

The final letter is **E** for Embodiment, which is about living, giving grace, and sharing what you've learned. With Embodiment, you embrace the understanding and belief that you already *are* the Future You — you're just practicing being her and getting better and better until it becomes a new set of habits or second nature.

The deeper rooted your healthy beliefs are — beliefs about your identity, your worth, your value — the less a traumatic situation is likely to affect you. You heal, and even more importantly, you become more resilient.

Obviously, practicing your new habits may still, at times, feel uncomfortable. You can't just do things like you used to. You will find yourself needing to stop, consider, and notice different opportunities that you might once have missed.

You will realize where your old thought habits were not helping you, and you'll learn to create new ones. Like all of the other parts of Healing TIME, this step keeps going, too. You get more comfortable doing the new and sometimes uncomfortable things, and then you find yourself doing more things to create the next version of Future You. With each new cycle of growth, you get more comfortable with being uncomfortable.

HOW THE COMPONENTS WORK TOGETHER

As a counseling professional, who has personally been healing for a long time (both prior to and during the years of therapy), I have read a lot of articles and books and have had many opportunities to attend workshops, seminars, and trainings. From what I have seen of other processes that deal with getting unstuck and healing, there are many things they don't focus on.

They often deal with only one part of a situation — the current mental or emotional situation, for instance. They don't necessarily look at the whole person from a past, present, and future standpoint. The Healing TIME approach is able to see the whole individual by combining therapeutic and coaching techniques.

Therapy is great for healing past grief, distress, and trauma. Yet not everyone who's trying to get unstuck needs therapy. When someone is stuck, it can mean they just don't have a way to see what's holding them back, and they need to work on it. And if they do need therapy, there's only so much that can be done through a book because therapy involves a relationship with another human.

If something you can't define feels as if it's holding you back and you are having a lot of trouble using the techniques in this book, therapeutic coaching or counseling may be more helpful prior to, or in tandem with this book, to work through your internal blocks in a healthy, safe way. I recommend finding a licensed therapist or a therapeutic coach to help you through that (if you would like to work with me, please see the ad in the back of the book).

However, if you just feel stuck and want to get somewhere different in your life, the Healing TIME method can help you do that by making the abstract more real. This is where Time comes in to help us see the past, present, and future as a connected set of elements that we can work with in different ways to create a new future.

Many Things Happen at Once

I believe we are interconnected (social), psychological, and spiritual beings. Consequently, healing usually needs to involve social/relational, mental/emotional, and spiritual aspects. This is what the Talk step offers. The support from Talk sets the foundation for Investigation (e.g., examining the information to try to predict if things will stay the same or change).

Once we have the data and a plan from Investigation, we're ready for Movement on the plan. The solid foundation we've laid from our support system in Talk and the info from Investigation helps us stick with the plan, which is vital because a lot of people don't make it that far.

However, it's important to note that even beginning the Investigation process is Movement. Movement is happening in different ways throughout the process. It's not linear, remember?

I'm not going to lie. This method is challenging. The difference between it and other things you may have tried is that the effort you make is going toward many different components at once, and it's also changing you in initially imperceptible ways. As you make progress and learn more about yourself and embodying the new you, you're actually rewiring your brain and body's neural connections. More on this later.

It's possible to achieve the wellness you want. The other great thing is that once you experience Healing TIME, it can continue to help you through every new cycle of growth and even become second nature in your day-to-day life.

Change Happens in Cycles

The interconnected aspect of the Healing TIME process shows how life is not linear. It is multidimensional and even cyclical. You rarely, if ever, finish one thing, tie it up in a nice little package, and then move on to the next. Everything is a work in progress.

The Healing TIME method thrives in this environment. It's common to work in several stages at the same time, as illustrated in Figure 4.1.

Figure 4.1 Time Spiral

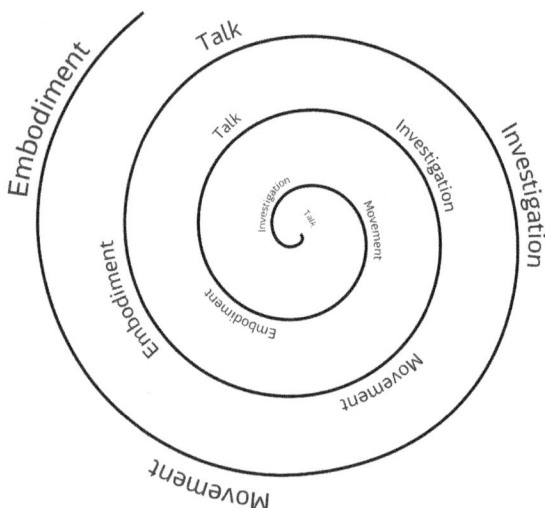

This was true for me. I didn't simply progress from one task to the next and keep moving forward. Each was intertwined with others.

We can be in multiple phases of this process at the same time. For instance, Talk and Movement work together because we are always going to need support while we are doing new things. The same is true for Investigation and Embodiment because we may need to reassess our plan to embody when we have new information. We continually evolve and change what we're doing as we navigate new life experiences.

LET'S START HEALING TIME

Now, it's time for you to put some of this into prac-tice for yourself. Right now, your goal is *learning*. We're about to start a new experiment, so be curious and ob-serve what happens.

Doesn't *just learning* feel more possible than *solving this problem*? I hope so. It did for me.

Now think about Time. How would you like Them to help you? Do you welcome and allow Them to help you see time as They do?

Some days, you will naturally feel more frustrated than others. You will feel like you didn't get where you were trying to go or that the goal is impossible. The dif-ference is that as you work through Healing TIME, you will accept these things as part of the process.

To get to where I was going, I had to accept that I was going to make mistakes and be gracious to my-self. No one usually gets things right the first time. That's why it's called learning — and learning can be so fun!

I've learned to laugh at myself in a loving way, with the affectionate sense that we're all humans doing our best to live life on this earth. Learning also takes time. When you're impatient with yourself and only focused on the end goal, you often forget to enjoy the journey of getting there.

Ready? Let's start the process.

LEARNING GOAL EXERCISE

Pick one value-related area from Chapter 1 that you want to work more on and set a goal related to it. The process will be a little different depending on whether you have (1) a specific challenge you're trying to solve or (2) a more nebulous set of challenges. Take some time and write about your goal. We'll use this as we move through the Healing TIME steps.

1. Specific Goal: Finding Your Ladder Rungs

If you have a specific goal, that's great. Let's get you closer to it. For now, though, try to visualize it as clearly as possible. For instance, if your goal is to overhaul your career, what would that look like? What does a day in your new career look like? Are you happy? Do you feel it's challenging? What kinds of people are you working with? And so forth.

In your notebook, write down why this goal is important and what it looks like for you. What does Future You have that you don't yet? Save extra pages for when you develop this vision more, which you will because you're committed to your healing! It will change and grow as you learn more from your experiences, just as you will change and grow.

The next step is to believe it is possible. You know where the ladder is going to take you — you just need to start discovering and/or creating those rungs. We'll do that in greater detail in the next few chapters. Are you willing to commit to your Future Self?

Assuming the answer is yes, now you're ready to start learning, so feel free to skip to the Write It Out section.

2. General Goal: Solidify the Nebulous

If you just want to feel better or be happier generally, your main goal is to start creating opportunities to make the abstract more concrete for yourself. To do this, pick a general values category from Chapter 1 that feels most interesting to you. It doesn't matter that you can't yet see how learning more about it will affect your life. Just go with your gut — what's calling to you? There may be more than one thing, which is great! If you have time to focus on more than one area, that's fine.

Remember: This isn't something you're going to solve. It's an area you're going to learn in and from. For instance, you could decide you're going to learn more about your own faith/spirituality through reading, reflection, and prayer. Or you could decide you're going to focus on your physical health by learning how to cook more nutritious meals and the type of movement you enjoy and your body needs. Whatever you choose is up to you.

Write It Out

In your notebook, write responses to the following questions:

- What made you choose this area?
- What things about this area are you interested in?
- What is the reason this is important to you?
- How do you plan on exploring this area?

Remember: This isn't a goal you're going to achieve and be done with — you're learning. Nobody is going to give you a test; you'll succeed when you apply what you learn. Progress, not perfection! As Andrea Liebross says, "B-minus work turned in is better than A-plus work that never gets turned in."[10]

CHAPTER 5

Healing Talk

*Don't spend most of your time on the voices that
don't count, voices that are going to add too little worth
to your future. Don't waste time on the shallow and
the silly. Tune those voices out and tune in voices
that are going to add something to your life.*

— JIM ROHN

Healing Talk is where everything begins. As motivational speaker, business consultant, and author Ed Rush wrote, "The key to changing the world is to first change your words."[11] This is so true.

In the Healing TIME framework, Talk includes all forms of communication — spoken, written, artistic, music, etc. What's most important is that you begin expressing your true feelings and thoughts. When this happens, you open yourself to new possibilities, which can then become reality.

Healing Talk has three components: Connect, Communicate, and Validate. In this chapter, we'll examine how these three things help you. You'll learn how to connect with yourself and others (including your higher power). You'll learn how to communicate your ideas and feel encouraged to listen to yourself and others. And you'll understand how Talk validates your experiences so you can achieve growth and healing.

What do these look like in your life?

Imagine yourself going about your day. You wake up, shower, and start the coffee machine. You walk back to pick out your outfit for the day, and BAM! You hit the side of your foot against the leg of a table. As waves of pain surge through your body, you yell in agony to release some of that painful energy, and you move and bounce to try and distract yourself.

After a few minutes, you settle down to assess the injury, realizing the pain isn't going away and might even be more than a bruise.

In this situation, you have different options for handling it. You may try to mask and ignore the pain so you can go on with your day. Unfortunately, the injury still exists. By ignoring it, you may just be doing more damage to yourself.

Another reaction could be to become overwhelmed, frozen, and helpless, as the pain and fear of the possibility of an injury keeps you from accomplishing anything else for the rest of the day.

A third option is to realize that the pain you feel could indicate a physical problem, and you may need help to fix it.

If you're the third type of person, your next step would be to connect with the right people, communicate your pain, and begin the process of validating your need for help to fix the injury. You go to the doctor and explain how the injury happened. The doctor confirms that a bone in your foot is broken and then helps to set it so it heals properly.

The third scenario seems reasonable for most. We get injured, we seek help, we get help, we understand what is going on, and we start healing. The process of healing emotional pain is similar, and Talk is the first step.

WHO CAN HELP YOU WITH YOUR PAIN?

Emotional pain can be as disruptive as physical pain. And yet, why do we struggle against reaching out for help when we experience emotional pain? We wouldn't do that with a physical injury.

However, our minds are more able to dismiss emotional grief and trauma. Because it's not something visible, many people try to ignore it or just muscle through it. Do you remember Marie, who was struggling with health problems? These also led to a myriad of emotional challenges.

When Marie finally found her spark of hope, she started to reach out to people other than medical professionals in order to expand her support network.

"I discovered there were many others in similar situations, and most importantly, I wasn't ALONE!" she said. "I was able to communicate my issues to others who spoke the same language and could really understand me."

The positive results came soon. A man named Robert responded to her request for help and not only completely validated her needs but also offered his services at no charge. He was an expert practitioner in the field but was now retired. "What a total Godsend this man was!" Marie exclaimed.

Robert taught her some specifics about how to best use her CPAP machine. "The best thing Robert did for me was to coach me through changing my thought patterns and shifting my mind's focus so I could overcome the panic and anxiety that had built up from all the choking and drowning I had been experiencing," Marie said.

These shifts required incremental steps. "Every night, before you fall asleep, put the mask on and go about your normal routine," Robert instructed. "Reading, watching television, listening to a podcast or music, whatever you do. Become familiar with the way the mask and air feel. Then, you can fall asleep knowing that you did fine with the mask on while you were awake." He explained how this would build her confidence.

"If, while wearing the mask, you wake up and feel like you're choking or drowning, simply and calmly take the mask off and take three slow, deep breaths. Tell yourself that you are okay and that you can **breathe**. Set the mask aside and go back to sleep," he advised. "When you wake up in the morning, take note that you were successful in wearing the mask for a period of time, regardless of the length. Three minutes or all night; it doesn't matter. It's about training the brain to build confidence in the process."

The next night, she was to repeat the process. "The key is to never give up," he told her. "Keep trying and applying the strategy. Success takes time. You're running a marathon, not a sprint."

Wow! These were such helpful instructions, and they truly changed Marie's life. They also reflect many of the core aspects of Healing TIME: building confidence in small steps, remaining calm, being compassionate toward yourself, retraining your brain and physical responses, and persevering for the long term rather than immediately deciding it doesn't work.

CONNECT

When you're isolated and alone, you may get caught in a loop — cycling through the same coping behaviors that aren't helping you. Marie's first step in Talk was to start creating some new connections beyond those she'd already tried. She was seeking new information and support.

My clients do this in two ways:

- Internally: through writing about their values, as I've already invited you to do in Chapter 1.
- Externally: through connecting and talking with others.

Reaching out to others can feel pretty scary at first. With practice, though, people are often surprised it gets easier and can even be fun.

It's also important you connect with people who will support you.

We Need People in Small and Large Ways

Healthy connections and communication are essential parts of the healing process, which makes sense because we are social beings. We need other people who help us feel safe and can be grounding agents in our lives.

Before being born, we are connected physically with our mothers. Both before and after birth, ideally, we have healthy connections with and feel safe and supported by one or more caregivers. As we grow and develop, we are likely to be connected with others — extended family, friends of family, friends we make, medical providers, spiritual leaders, community, and so on.

Those are ideals. We may or may not have a healthy family. However, while that's not up to us, we can build our own emotionally safe support system of people.

There are people who have the capacity to care for us in helpful, beneficial ways. Isolating yourself because you're afraid to be vulnerable with your emotional hurt is akin to living with a broken bone or chronic disease. You do not seek help because your fear of being dismissed or misunderstood has become greater than your drive to get help to fix and/or change the problem. That only leaves you stuck, sick, hurt, and alone. Consider that you may need to be vulnerable with different people outside of your "normal" circles in order to build the support system you need.

Unfortunately, it's not always easy to be vulnerable and connect. Sometimes, we assume no one cares, or maybe we are hurt by past experiences with people. This can keep us closed off from opportunities to find connection, and others may not even know we're seeking connection.

Marie told me a relatable example of this habit of assuming others don't care. One day, as she was at the eye doctor's office and they were discussing her vision, he asked, "How is it going, managing your diabetes?"

Thinking he was just asking a clinical question, she gave him a short answer. Yet, with a kind smile, he pressed her a little more. "Have any of the changes you've made helped? Are you feeling stressed out about it?"

Marie was surprised. She realized he really cared about her as another human; he wasn't just making a clinical diagnosis. They went on to have a great conversation in which they both shared ways they dealt with stress, and he was just as interested in her experience as she was in his.

If she hadn't cared for her health and had instead remained closed off due to her assumption, she'd have missed that opportunity to connect.

Make Your Connections

People who care are all around you.

If you walk into your hair salon and your stylist, who has been cutting your hair for ten years, tells you he notices you look tense and asks you if everything's okay, it's because he knows you and cares about you. You don't have to tell him everything in your life, but perhaps you can confide a little to him.

These small connections have a lot of power to help you feel supported. Your server at your favorite restaurant, the grocery cashier whose line you often find yourself in, the bank teller, any of these people could be a small connection.

Of course, you probably also want closer friends whom you can trust with anything. Those kinds of friends are found by being open and also by reaching out to them. If you have a spiritual practice, connecting with your higher power definitely needs to be included, and those who share the same beliefs may also be good connections.

If you feel like you don't have anyone, that's also beneficial information. Let's work together to start finding some people!

Here are some things to do (I have heard real stories of success for each of these categories below):

- Look through your list of friends, maybe on social media or in your phone contacts. Is there anyone on it who you can reach out to who shares your values and interests? Is there anyone who could just be there to listen? You could even start small by just discussing your shared interests.
- Find interest-based groups where you can connect with people in your area. What do you enjoy doing? Board games, hiking, Harry Potter, pickleball, etc.
- Follow your interests by finding podcasters, YouTubers, or bloggers and start following them. You may not have conversations with them, but they are connections and people who care. Among their followers, you might connect with others who can help you feel more seen.
- Search for interest-based social media groups (like Marie found). These can align with your goals and generally have good guidelines in place to make sure interactions are supportive.
- Limit unhealthy connections. It's equally important to identify connections that don't

help/serve you. Is there anyone in your life you need to limit connection with? How can you set those boundaries?

Try making one connection this week and see how it goes.

If there are any connections you need to limit, work on how to do that. For example, one of my clients, Cora, realized she needed to spend less time with her mom, Vicki. While Cora loved her mom, Vicki could be demanding and critical, and it wasn't a healthy relationship. With her support system, Cora was able to clarify how much time felt healthy to spend with Vicki and what kinds of behavior she could and couldn't be around. She changed the connection so that it supported her needs.

COMMUNICATE

Communication is not always easy. Take my coaching client — let's call her Fran — who came to me with a lot of frustrations about her work situation and her career in general. During the intake process, she explained that she was working way too many hours, and she didn't know how to deal with the situation. The main problem was that she felt her boss wasn't aware of how much he was piling on her (and other high achievers in the office).

As we began to work through her situation, I realized Fran was hesitant to communicate directly with her boss to set some boundaries.

"We have a good relationship, but he can sometimes take things personally," she told me. "I don't know how to tell him I've got too much work without sounding like a complainer or like I'm mad at him."

As a result, she took work home every night, although she didn't tell her boss. She would make dinner for her family, and then, when the kids were in bed, she would pull out her laptop and work at the kitchen table to finish up what she hadn't gotten done at the office.

Her husband had taken a second shift job last year, so he was rarely there for dinner. Fran felt alone and overwhelmed. They hadn't realized last year that she'd have this much work. It had somehow just crept up to this level. Now, without her husband's help with the kids every evening, she was getting tired, and their relationship was suffering.

After more coaching, she finally talked to her husband and told him how overwhelmed she felt. She was grateful to have his emotional support, though there were no positions left on the day shift for him to take at the moment. She also reestablished connections with some of her old friends, and she joined a women's group online where she found other women who felt a lot like she did. Suddenly, she started figuring out some solutions to her problems. Others had been there, and they were able to give her some good suggestions when she asked for them.

She was surprised to learn some of them struggled with the same things and totally understood how she felt. One of her mentors at the office was especially helpful in giving her some ideas for gaining confidence. Fran was blown away that this other woman, who was in a higher position in a different department, would take time to care about Fran's struggles. Just knowing that gave Fran more confidence and motivation.

Through communication, Fran eventually developed a support network where she felt safe and could work through her challenges. She commiserated with women in similar situations, obtained advice from a trusted mentor, and shared her worries with her spouse. These interactions gave her a solid foundation and built up her confidence so she could talk to her boss — a step we'll discuss later in the book.

Sharing Your Goal Helps You Achieve It

Communication can be used for support, but it's also a way to hold yourself accountable. Who in your life knows what you want for yourself? Who knows what changes you want to make?

As you build and strengthen your network, be brave and share things with them. Does your support team, including your therapist (if applicable), know your goal? Have you communicated it to your higher power (if applicable)?

Speaking of higher powers, did you know that when you share a goal with someone you perceive as having a higher status or being more accomplished in that area, you're more likely to achieve the goal?[12]

The following may sound crazy, but it's not. Visualizing different elements of yourself as independent "people/roles" and knowing how each feels and thinks is important. Are there any parts of you (thoughts, emotions, younger versions of yourself) that aren't aware of what the main part of you wants? Is your entire self in agreement with it?

If not, have you listened to these different parts to find out why? Have you shared your *why* with the whole you? We can be in conflict with ourselves if we don't communicate within.

Communicate Your Goal

Here's your task for this week:

- Communicate the learning goal (specific or general) you decided on in Chapter 4 to one person this week.
- Remember to also communicate your wishes about what you need from that person in relation to the goal. "I just need you to listen" or "I need to get some advice" are perfectly reasonable requests.

See how things go and then decide what you learned.

VALIDATE

Validation means being seen, understood, and acknowledged in the past and present. One of Fran's biggest sources of pain was that she didn't feel validated in her work situation.

Part of this was because she was isolating herself when what she really needed were more connections. Once she made those connections — with the right people — she started to feel better because she realized she wasn't the only one feeling like she did. Feeling seen and understood gave Fran newfound confidence.

Validation Leads to Change

Validation doesn't mean you think someone is right or wrong. It's about communicating to the other person that you hear them and accept their feelings as they are now. As a therapist, I may validate a client's experience to help them feel heard and understood. However, my acceptance of their thoughts and corresponding emotions doesn't mean every thought and emotion they have is accurate or healthy. It means I understand and empathize with where they are right now, and I accept that as a fact of their subjective experience.

When we feel heard and understood, we are more willing to let down our wall of protection or defense, and that allows us to do what is needed to make the necessary changes.

When we don't feel heard and understood, we don't want to listen to someone else or even ourselves. If you've ever been in a friendship or a romantic relationship with someone who doesn't seem to understand you and accept who you are, how willing were you to do something different for that person? What credibility do they have in asking for change from you if they don't even demonstrate that they know you?

Validate Yourself

One of our first sources of validation needs to be ourselves.

Let's face it: We can be our own worst critics. When we want something, we often tell ourselves we shouldn't. We may tell ourselves our feelings are stupid or that doing something is a waste of time. We may tell ourselves the pain in our foot is no big deal and then take medicine to mask it so we can go about our day without thinking about what we're doing to ourselves. For whatever reason, we just assume that's what we're supposed to do.

Communication plays a gentle but powerful role in feeling seen and understood, starting with the way we talk to ourselves. Do you overtly or covertly dismiss, avoid, berate, or curse yourself, your thoughts, beliefs, emotions, or tears? Or do you validate the sadness, frustration, and confusion because it is where you are and what you are feeling?

Compassionate self-talk is crucial for positive growth and change. Research by Kristin Neff strongly correlates self-compassion with positive well-being.[13] If we don't validate ourselves, it may be more difficult to find others who will, too. I can't give you a task to get validation from someone else, as that relies on them. However, here are some ways to show yourself this kindness.

- Tell yourself three validating statements. These can relate to struggles you're having with your learning goal or any pain you may be experiencing. Some examples include:
  o "I get that this is really frustrating, and you've been trying things for a long time."
  o "It's okay to feel like taking a break. How can you do that without giving up?"
  o "I know this has been a painful experience for you. You've been hurt, and you need some time to heal."
- Be mindful of opportunities where you can show others you see and understand them. When they express their own concerns, let them know you hear them. (However, if you're prone to people-pleasing actions, be cautious about overdoing this.)
- If you feel you need more validation from members of your support network, communicate your request to them and clarify what you mean so they understand.

If we cannot be honest (with compassion) to ourselves about where we are — which is validation — then it's going to be really difficult to move out of our current state to achieve our goals. That's why Validate is such a crucial part of Talk. Without it, Talk can potentially undermine you rather than support you.

BE MINDFUL OF YOUR TALK

Now that you've seen how Healing Talk works, you can start working on it by being more present in the current moment. You can notice if the messages you're giving and receiving are ones that support and validate both yourself and others.

What can start this process of self-reflection and recognizing our self-talk through mindfulness? An example is unplugging while walking in the park, noticing the details of the world around you through your senses or through a guided meditation.

Time, your constant companion, can help by letting you know when you're not supporting the values you cherish. This will help you solidify your goals, and you'll build the rungs of your ladder much faster and more effectively.

CHAPTER 6

Healing Investigation

To achieve great things, two things are needed:
a plan and not quite enough time.

— LEONARD BERNSTEIN

The Investigation step is a crucial part of the Healing TIME process. It is where we uncover our underlying problems as well as the fears that keep us from facing them. It is also where we will discover ways to work through those fears and discover new opportunities.

Once you understand your inner landscape, you can then question and challenge limiting beliefs, doubts, assumptions, and fears, clearing the way to focus on new possibilities. To move you toward achieving your intended goal, we'll explore the three components of Investigation: Assess, Plan, and Prepare.

Getting to the Investigation stage can take a little time. Consider Fran, who mentioned how she was having panic attacks at work because of the daily pressure she was experiencing.

Our initial meetings focused on the ways she had been trying to mitigate her workload — becoming more efficient, managing her time by grouping tasks, and implementing other organizational strategies. After our conversations, it became apparent that time management was not her issue, and I decided we needed to ask more questions.

What would it look like a year from now — five years, even ten — if nothing changed? (I first heard this question from healthcare consultant Frank Benedetto with The Honey Badger Project[14]; I love it because it always surprises people.)

Fran looked stunned. "Well, I guess... I guess I'll be doing this. That's a really depressing thought. I don't even want to think about it."

"Okay. I want you to push a little further into the 'I can't even stand to think about it' because that's going to motivate you to get where you want to go. So, if you were to think about it even a little — say a year from now — what would it look like?"

She sighed. "I'll be way more tired. I'll probably have health issues. I'm already having panic attacks. I already don't have time to have friendships or anything else because I'm constantly either working or doing stuff for my family, so I don't get enough sleep. I'm sure that's not good for me."

"It's good that you recognize your health could be impacted," I said. "Sometimes, we have a one-track mind and just keep plowing away. So, I hear you want to rest, you want to feel healthy, you want to connect with people who you care about, and you want to feel a little happier."

"Yeah, I want a life other than just working."

"Do you like your job?" I asked her. "You've mentioned you want to do something different."

She paused. "I guess — I mean, in some ways, yes. I really like the people there. I'm just not sure about the work. I've actually thought about... maybe a different job. I just don't know what."

My curiosity was piqued. It was clear she valued her family time and her relationships, yet she wasn't setting boundaries that would protect that time from her work. And underneath, she wasn't sure the job she had was right for her. She had started out in our sessions by spinning between "Things are fine at work for now" and "I'm working too much," but now she was spinning between "Things are fine at work for now" and "I wish I could do something different."

The problem was she didn't have any idea what she would rather do. She needed to start creating more opportunities to find out.

It was time for her to begin the Investigation phase.

BUILD YOUR LIFE ON SOLID GROUND

Have you ever built a house or a structure of some sort? One of the first steps in the process involves investigating the land that will support the structure. It's essential to determine if there are any flaws that need to be fixed and then prepare the land to support the structure.

The same is true when we are building ourselves into the best version we can be or planting new seeds of change in our lives. We need to spend some time investigating our own internal "land" to see what needs to be prepared or changed.

The challenge is that fear or assumptions often prevent us from investigating those rough places (also called shadow parts or blind spots) within ourselves, which can result in building on ground that may have hidden issues.

Remember how Marie stood on her porch looking at the storm damage and the broken trees left behind? One of those trees was a beautiful olive tree planted over a decade before. It had grown tall and looked healthy. Now, this tree was broken and in pieces on the ground. Why?

While cleaning up, Marie discovered the olive tree had been planted on a portion of land where the soil beneath the surface was mostly sand — loose and unstable, leaving the roots without the support needed to take hold. If only the person who had planted it had investigated the soil, they might have been able to improve it or plant the tree elsewhere. Either choice could have given the tree the strength it needed to survive the storm.

Investigation is a crucial step toward moving forward and getting the results we want. In fact, it can even be a useful way to figure out what we want.

For instance, until Fran figured out what she really wanted, she was trying to take action without a true goal — she wasn't even sure what foundation she was building her "house (life)" on. As a result, she wasn't getting anywhere. Continuing on that path would eventually lead to burnout, resentment, and other negative results that could be avoided simply by digging more deeply into the situation.

ASSESS

The first part of Healing Investigation requires figuring out your current situation. This includes recognizing existing behaviors, learning new ways to respond to situations, and connecting all of this information so you can find new opportunities and ways to move forward.

When assessing your current situation, you are looking at that information with questions in mind. What opportunities are here? What new things have I learned that could change things? What sorts of changes can I make based on this information? What is my next step?

Assessment also includes recognizing the methods you use to interact with the past, present, and future and then reflecting on whether those are successful.

During consultation calls with new clients, I ask them to share what caused them to seek out counseling and what things in their lives they would like to be different. Often, they share a bit about their past, including their childhood. My questions are all part of assessing where someone is, where they've been, and how they would like to shape their future. By using assessment tools, I can start looking at their internal "landscape" and become better prepared to help them achieve their intended goals for the future.

Assessing Information, Habits, and Methods

As you gather information, make connections, and investigate potential opportunities, you're creating new knowledge and approaches that will help you change.

Assessment requires being mindful and should include an element of self-reflection. To this end, you can also assess your methods for gathering information and how you're responding to it. How is your investigation changing your assumptions? What new things have you learned?

For example, if you're trying something new related to fitness, how is it going? What do you **notice** about your body's responses? How about your emotional ones? Are your beliefs supportive, or do you find they're challenging your progress? Is the way you view your goal motivating you?

I learned something funny about this process when I decided I wanted to learn Spanish. I had tried learning it before, but I quit. I tried it again. And I quit again. This cycle happened way too many times.

Then, one day, I realized I didn't want to *learn* Spanish. Learning a language was challenging work. I just wanted to *know* Spanish. Obviously, I wasn't going to just know it without the work, but my "aha!" moment came when I figured out the actual problem: I wanted it to be fun, and it wasn't.

A language coach taught me to look at learning from a place of curiosity and to have fun. What a concept! That changed everything. Now, I just practice for fun; it's not a goal that I have to work at or achieve by a certain time. Now, I'm learning *and* knowing Spanish without it feeling like a burden. It's just happening while I play a game. I even added Swedish because I thought, "Why not?" I have been able to practice both languages in countries that predominately speak it.

That's what I mean when I tell you it's important to have fun. When looking at this as serious work all the time, it gets heavy. It becomes more weight you're adding to your metaphorical backpack. The heavier that pack gets, the more difficulty you have getting up that next rung, and the more tempting it is to quit climbing.

TOP THREE FEARS MY CLIENTS EXPRESS

After more than a decade of working with clients, I've noticed that their fears often fall into three main categories. Do any of these sound like you?

1. **Fear of Rejection or Disapproval:** You worry about setting boundaries, saying no, or making decisions that prioritize your own needs above those of others because you don't want to disappoint or alienate them. This fear often comes from a belief that your value is tied to how others view you, such as whether you're helpful, capable, or agreeable.

2. **Fear of Making the Wrong Decision:** You feel paralyzed by the idea that your choices will lead to failure, regret, or negative consequences. This leads to overthinking and procrastination as you try to control every possible outcome. This fear often comes from the belief that mistakes are unforgivable while perfection is possible and expected.

3. **Fear of Being Seen as Weak or Selfish:** You worry that asking for help, setting limits, or prioritizing your well-being will make you appear incapable or self-centered. This fear often comes from your belief that you are expected to "handle it all" without burdening others.

Assessing Root Beliefs

What thoughts and fears do you have about yourself and your desired goal? Knowing these can keep you from self-sabotage.

To help clients begin to assess their root beliefs, I like to use an exercise that asks them to describe things that are going on and then identify the personal meaning they attach to those events. Specifically, what do they think those events say about them? That's how I began with Fran. The discussion looked like this:

Me: "What do you believe leaving your current job might say about you?"

Fran: "That I'm giving up."

Me: "What do you believe giving up might say about you?"

Fran: "Well… that I'm wishy-washy, I guess. Or not committed."

Me: "And what do you believe that might say about you?"

Fran: "That I don't have enough discipline."

Me: "And what do you believe that might say about you?"

Fran: "That I just need to change my attitude."

Me: "And what do you believe that might say about you?"

Fran: "That I am lazy."

Me: "And what do you believe that might say about you?"

Fran: "That I'm not good enough to work there. That I'm worthless and can't stick to things when they get tough."

Identifying those types of underlying beliefs can make a huge difference in your progress.

Root beliefs are beliefs that permeate the majority of your life. These are the ground you're building on. Like the sandy ground in Marie's yard, some of our root beliefs leave us standing on unstable ground.

Fran feared leaving her job might mean she was undisciplined. She feared that speaking up might mean she was a complainer. And yet, there was no evidence that those were true. They were just ideas and fears. Spinning back and forth between them was keeping her from getting to the next rung of her belief ladder.

THE WEIGHT IN YOUR BACKPACK

I always used to carry a backpack (affectionately referred to by my colleagues as my turtle shell because it was always so full of stuff). I often didn't even use anything in the bag. Nevertheless, I carried it like I carried my mental and emotional burdens: on my shoulders and everywhere I went.

Turtle shells are the turtle's protection. That's exactly how my backpack felt to me. It was stuff I *might* need. The fact that I mostly didn't need it — well, that didn't matter. I might need it sometime.

Root beliefs are like that backpack. Imagine you're standing on a ladder, and you're about to climb up the next rung. No big deal, right? It's one step.

Except in this case, you've got a backpack strapped to your back containing all your worldly possessions. You've got to climb this ladder carrying all this stuff because... well, you're not sure. It's stuff you've always had. It's stuff you might need.

The trip up each step of that ladder looks (and feels) pretty tough. That backpack is heavy. You have to rest a lot between rungs. Whew! You wish you could take that thing off, but what if you need something in there and you don't have it? Hey, it could happen!

When we're dealing with beliefs, they either help us move forward or hold us back. When they're like weights we're carrying around in a backpack, they hold us back. We have to sort through them to see what we really need and what we're just carrying around for a sense of protection.

Assess Yourself

You probably have some core or root beliefs you don't quite know how to face. Most of us do, and they can affect us without our knowing it.[15]

These beliefs can often manifest as what psychiatrist and brain disorder specialist Dr. Daniel Amen calls ANTs, or automatic negative thoughts.[16] ANTs are unwanted, unhelpful thoughts that can be overly self-critical, complaining, or despairing. If we don't stop them, they will multiply — just like ants. Your entire internal dialogue will be overrun by them. If you've ever had an ant infestation in your garden, you know what I mean.

Let's start decolonizing the ANT population before it takes hold even more. Here's a task to assess your ANT situation:

- Take a moment to try the root belief exercise. Think of something you feel you have to keep doing but don't really want to. Try to make it something related to your goal. For instance, "I have to go to every one of my kid's sporting events."
  - What do you believe that says about you? Maybe you feel it is a sign you're a good parent.
  - If you don't do it, what do you believe that says about you? Say you miss one or two games. Do you interpret that to mean you're a bad parent? Delve more deeply and ask again: What do you believe that might say about you?
  - Keep questioning yourself until you reach what feels like a root belief. Sometimes, during this process, emotions may arise. If so, that is your body communicating something.

It's nothing to be afraid of; you're just learning your body's language, which you may not be as familiar with *yet*. Again, if it feels like you don't have coping tools, please pause or skip for now. This could be something to work on in counseling.

- How has this root belief affected your life?
- Is this belief really true? Do you know when you internalized it? How old does that internalized belief feel? When did that part hear it or come to believe it? If it's too distressing or you can't remember, that's okay. It's just another way to validate where you are now, but it's not crucial.
- If you want to try to identify the main root/core beliefs you have (positive or negative) by looking at a list of common ones I've put together, you can find it through the Resources link at the back of the book.

PLAN

Once you've assessed your root beliefs and how they influence your actions, you can begin to put together a more concrete plan and start adding rungs to your ladder that aren't limited by those beliefs.

Remember, creating these rungs starts with belief. I know it's odd to stand at the bottom of a ladder with most of its rungs missing and think about being at the top. You'd like to just teleport yourself up there.

The key resides in Future You. If you can see at least part of their situation more clearly now, you'll be able to begin to figure out how to reverse engineer the ladder to get to the top.

Let's use a fitness example. Suppose I know I want good physical health. What does that mean to me? I decide it means Future Me is active and strong. She has fun walking with friends, participates in local fun runs, and has more than enough energy to do her daily work and live a full life.

That's at the top of the ladder, right? Now, I can start reverse engineering those things by going backward, step by step, to see how Future Me got there.

So, before she (remember this is Future Me) got to that top rung, what was she able to do? Yes, she had some small health issues, AND (note how this is *and* vs. *but* here because there's no hesitation — words are important!) she knew how to treat them. She was keeping up with her work and personal life, though she didn't have too much energy to spare at the end of the day. She was diligently active, yet maybe not for as long as she liked, and she wasn't always totally ready for more.

So, on the rung beneath "almost to the top," there's a step down — maybe that step is general health. The next one down might be energy, then exercise, and so on, until after several rungs, we get to the present moment.

You can measure each rung however you wish; the most important thing is that each one progressively moves you toward Future You and that they include both specific and general goals. In this way, they can be broken into manageable chunks. I can look at the interim steps and decide how to attain them or adjust them. Maybe I need more steps (or fewer). I also need to start thinking realistically about how long it's going to take to reach each new rung and adjust my expectations along the way.

When I am finished setting these goals, I have my plan!

At times, your goals may be more abstract, yet it's still possible to create concrete steps to attain them. Think about Fran. Her goals were mostly internal, so we focused on them in relation to how she would feel and what she would believe about herself from the top all the way down. On the top rung, she's confident and happy, believes she can do whatever she sets her mind to, and enjoys her life. One step down, she has a few doubts sometimes, yet mostly deals with them quickly. A step down from that, she has some doubts and isn't always sure how to proceed. However, she knows how to figure it out and who to talk to, and she feels able to tackle them. And so on, working her way down the ladder to where she is now.

Create Your Own Plan

You might not be ready to create a full plan yet, but you can start to make one for the goal you set in Chapter 4.

- Start with your final outcome and reverse engineer until you get to your current situation.
- Look at the steps, decide if they're incremental enough or too small/big and adjust as needed.
- Start looking at a timeline these steps might require and decide what expectations are realistic.
- What beliefs and feelings are coming up as you look at your plan? How can you address doubts or feelings of hopelessness if they arise?
- If mindfulness is not listed, I highly encourage you to look into different forms that may be more aligned with your preferences. Tara Brach says, "The gift of mindfulness [is] when we can be with

what's here, then we bring clarity and kindness to it. We find there is space for it and are no longer in reactivity to it... That shift in identity is the whole deal because then we can respond with wisdom."[17]

- If you need help with these steps, check in with your support system. And sometimes the internet (with caution) can help.

PREPARE

When you have a plan, you have a much more concrete idea of what you need to do next. You know more about what resources you'll need to devote toward it, what equipment you might need, and who you might need to ask for help. You may need to buy some tangible things — like fitness equipment, for example.

What about your mental equipment? That's just as important.

Once you have a plan, be diligent about not falling back on old belief systems. Instead of thinking about all the ways things can go wrong or how impossible it feels, focus on your preparation and plan — your step-by-step guide to get to Future You. While it won't happen in one fell swoop, you're steadily working toward your goal.

Plans are about the future, and the future can feel like a scary place. We don't have control because we don't know what will happen. We could fail. These are common fears, and it helps to expect them and prepare for them.

Facing Fears

Something I like to do with clients is to help them take power over their future by investigating the worst-case scenario.

Here's an example: One of my clients has a fear of flying in a plane, and it's preventing him from achieving several of his goals — for both career and personal travel.

"What's the worst thing that could happen?" I gently asked him.

"Well, dying," he said. "That seems pretty bad."

"All right," I replied. "What's the worst thing about dying?"

Surprised, he replied, "Um... well, I won't get to see those I love or do the things I dreamed of doing."

"And what's the worst thing about that?" I asked.

"I won't make an impact on anyone in my life," he said, tears filling his eyes. "I'll be forgotten."

"And what's the worst thing about that?" I gently asked again.

"I won't have any value," he replied, now totally deflated.

"All right," I said. "How does your current situation allow you to have more value than you would if you were dead?"

He paused. "Well — I'm here with my family."

"You've said your fear of flying is causing you to give up a big promotion," I said. "How could that promotion bring more value to your family?"

"Well, I've been wanting to move us to a bigger house," he said. "My girls have to share a room right now. The oldest just turned fourteen, and she's frustrated she has to share her room with an eight-year-old. When she has friends over for sleepovers, they have to sleep in the living room."

"So, your fear of flying is preventing you from doing something that will make you and others happier — make an impact on them?"

"I suppose so."

"If you never get over your fear of flying, what will happen?" I asked him.

"Nothing would change. I have to travel for this other job I want, but I'd be stuck where I am. I... I might not even be able to pay for my kids' college," he said. "At least, not all of it." He realized he wouldn't be able to take his kids on trips to interesting places if they couldn't drive to get there. The list started to grow.

As we went on and he started comparing the likelihood of dying against the surety of never getting to do the other things he wanted to do, he began to realize how much his fear was actually undermining his ability to do more for his family. He also accepted that a plane wasn't the only place where he could die. As all of this became clearer, it was the motivation he needed to try flying. It wasn't magic — he had a lot more work to do to get over the fear, including experiential trauma therapy on the root cause. However, he was willing to take the steps to do it.

What's Your "Worst Thing"?

Everyone's worst thing is different. A more common example would be someone's fear of public speaking. The worst thing about that for one person might be that he'd make a fool of himself, while for another person, it could be that she would fail to make her points and therefore feel like a failure. Feeling foolish or like a failure is about judgment, and the worst thing about that may be thinking, "I am not good enough."

Once you understand what the worst thing is for you, your plan can include ways to overcome the fears and assumptions. It's important to be 100 percent honest with yourself here so you don't get stuck.

Did you notice that part of Prepare is still going back and forth between Plan and Assess? This is another example of how this process isn't linear. The different dimensions affect each other.

This set of tasks is asking you to be courageous.

- You know in your head (cognitively) but not yet in your heart (belief) that it's worth it. So, what is the worst thing about working through the stuck place you're in?
- What is the worst thing about trying to get unstuck?
- What is the worst thing about NEVER getting unstuck?

Almost always, what makes an experience feel like the worst thing isn't just the situation itself. It's the emotion we feel about it and how that shows up in your body and mind.

Some clients, like Marie, say something like, "The worst thing is that it is not possible; this is just the way it is." If you're in this state of mind, the feeling can seem like apathy, but there's something else under it — perhaps sadness or even hopelessness. And others, like Fran, feel as if they will be worthless.

I do not want anyone to feel their life is doomed to be hopeless or that they are worthless. Even if there are things that can't be changed about a situation, other things can be added and shifted. And no person is worthless, no matter their abilities or limitations. Everyone has value; everyone can make a contribution somewhere.

If you don't know your value, investigate. Ask. Learn. And most importantly, believe.

TIMELINE EXTENSION EXERCISE

Remember that timeline of positive and negative events? Let's get it out and look at the endpoint — where you were when you created it. That right side of the paper was the end of the timeline at that point in time.

Now, get out a new sheet of paper and tape it on the back to the previous one so that you have a whole new blank sheet ahead of the place where you were. What do you want that space to be filled with? Draw a line from the previous "you are here" endpoint, forward toward the end of the new extended sheet (see Figure 6.1).

Above the line, where the positive/pleasant experiences go, write out what types of things Future You is experiencing. These don't have to be plotted in a specific timeframe like in the example; they just have to be there somewhere. These are the things your future can hold if you keep going. Sure, there will probably be some negative events since that's how we can recognize things that are positive/pleasant. However, Future You knows how to deal with the negative things because she's been practicing a lot of new beliefs and building neural pathways to learn the new skills she needs.

Figure 6.1 Timeline Extension

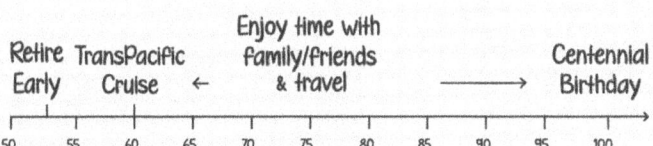

This is where your plan is taking you.

Now, where you had the "You Are Here" moment, draw a line down the middle dividing Past You from Future You. This is your boundary. This is where you can start removing the baggage of Past You and begin heading up the ladder.

Ready for the next step? Let's go!

CHAPTER 7

Healing Movement

Time flies. It's up to you to be the navigator.
— **ROBERT ORBEN**

In the Movement portion of our process, we explore how you can take small steps and challenge yourself in new ways that **align** with your goals and values. We'll discuss how you can evaluate what is true or untrue about how you view barriers that come up. Movement involves four components: Step, Challenge, Reevaluate, and Unify.

Several years ago, I had a client, Jordan, who had been through a traumatic, near-death car accident. Miraculously, Jordan made it out alive but not without permanent injury and chronic pain. In addition to his physical injuries, Jordan was terrified of getting behind the wheel of a car again. His fears were so strong that he started to build a metaphorical wall, and the longer he went without driving, the higher that wall became.

We discussed the reasons why he needed to work toward breaking down that wall. Rather than try to take on the entire barrier all at once, he needed to just try one small step at a time. Just remove one brick.

I asked Jordan what he thought he could do to begin. What would removing one brick look like? Jordan decided that when he got home, he would just try sitting in the driver's seat.

I reminded him to recognize this as a big step and to approach it with an open mindset. I suggested he repeat a phrase to keep himself focused on the moment — "I am safe; I am capable; It's okay to have emotions." On that day, Jordan accomplished his goal.

Over the next few weeks, he was able to put the keys in the ignition and then start the car. Next, he drove down his street. At this point, Jordan was proud of his progress and undertook additional trauma therapy to help him directly address the root cause of his fears so he could continue to move forward. Eventually, he could drive on the highway to the store. With each brick he removed, Jordan's confidence and hope grew, and now that wall is completely deconstructed.

Let's go back to the broken foot analogy. Remember the person who sought help right away and confirmed their foot was broken? That person's choice to get help was their one small step — the first brick removed that led to the intended goal.

We need to take that tiny step to spark hope and motivation. From there, we can continue to challenge ourselves to accomplish things that we previously did not believe were possible and then build on that foundation.

~~TRY~~ – STEP

The first component of Movement is Step. You'll notice that I've included "try" but crossed it out. People sometimes assume that this first phase involves just testing the waters — giving it a try before really diving in. However, "try" doesn't feel committed. The Step component is truly a step — maybe even out of your comfort zone. When you take a true Step, you're willing to experience what happens, and whatever the result is, you don't see it as a failure. It's just a step, and you're learning from the results.

The Step component is when we move forward and begin to experience the success we want and have planned for. However, this is often another point where people get stuck, usually because of existing fears.

To prevent those fears from slowing your progress, remember the Plan phase. You've prepared for this moment. You're not teleporting straight to the goal; you have a ladder with steps to get there. You've made the steps closer together when needed because you will make progress by creating little wins and celebrating them.

Start Small and Celebrate Often

We are thrilled when a baby rolls over, crawls, stands, or takes one step. It's a great reminder of how beneficial it is to create and celebrate little wins. Once you have one win, it can create a cascade of other positive steps and wins (the domino effect). Sometimes, for me, celebrating can be just simply telling someone else what I've done, like someone in my support system.

Unfortunately, as adults, we can be quick to dismiss these little wins, but they are vital if you've been stuck. Not allowing yourself to celebrate may actually be one reason why you're stuck.

According to performance coach Brendon Burchard, founder of the High Performance Institute, when we measure ourselves with impossibly high standards and don't acknowledge any of our successes along the way, we can sabotage our confidence. "Your self-concept stopped at a trauma. Your self-concept stopped at a bad day... at a certain income level... at a business level... at a divorce... And after it, you had all these wins... all these successes... but none of them got in there. You don't feel stronger because you ain't puttin' nothing in there!"[18] We need to integrate these wins into our self-concept, or we remain stuck in outdated, non-factual ideas of ourselves.

Remember: If you want your life to change, you can't keep thinking the same way. If you feel uncomfortable celebrating, try to just recognize the feeling of accomplishment — even if the feeling is teensy-tiny. It should still be celebrated! Acknowledge your change.

You've Already Taken Steps

Guess what? The goal you started with was a type of Step. And if you've done the exercises up to this point, you have created a plan. See how it works? You've already done this!

Still, I'm not going to let you off the hook without a task for this section. However, I believe this one will cause you to smile:

- Celebrate. Yes, pat yourself on the back for a moment here. You've already taken *several* steps. You already have a plan!
- Try celebrating with some verbal affirmations. "I am making progress." "I am on my way toward the future I want."

Maybe celebrations and affirmations feel uncomfortable. That's normal at first. And isn't that discomfort better than the discomfort of depression or hopelessness? Believe me, the emotions awaiting you on the flip side of this process are worth some discomfort.

Imagine feeling proud and hopeful and even laughing at how things used to be. That may still be in the future a bit — you have a few more rungs to go — ~~but~~ AND (real edit left in because words have power) I want you to know it is possible.

CHALLENGE

Taking a step is a challenge in itself. Now, though, let's take it a little further and do something that feels a little scarier. There's a reason for this.

When you take on and accomplish a challenge, even despite fear or self-criticism, you create new beliefs. These beliefs often begin to integrate confidence, clarity, compassion, resilience, and more into your being.

They **rewrite** those neural pathways we talked about. You'll be more resilient and better equipped to handle the pain and challenges of life, such as loss of employment, relationship conflicts, or the death of a loved one.

Here's another way to rewrite those pathways as well. Because I lived so much in my head, I was often disconnected from my body; Talk and Investigation let me stay in my head while slowly connecting to the body in a titrated way. This allowed me to be more ready for the mind, body, and spirit healing that has happened through the years via massage and craniosacral sessions (a type of gentle touch therapy for the central nervous system, including the skull and other bones, soft tissues, and cerebrospinal fluid), and recently I have begun using a vibroacoustic table (Zencora) for myself and clients. These modalities, along with Somatic Experiencing (another body-focused therapy, often used to help heal trauma) and similar body-based healing, can help reduce inflammation and facilitate the nervous system learning to regulate more, thereby becoming more resilient.

These body-based healing practitioners in my life through the last 11 years have also been a significant part of my support system from Talk. I realized I needed different people for different seasons of healing in my life. Body-based healing is also called the bottom-up approach (Dr. Bruce Perry) and leads us to the next point about getting back to our beginnings.

Build a Better Cognitive Template

As you think about a challenge, try thinking like a baby. No, I'm not kidding. Hear me out.

When adults try new things, we often approach these experiences with a mix of curiosity (often very small) and the negative, unhealthy programming of our past. The latter often includes fear and a negative inner critic. Remember those ANTs, those automatic negative thoughts?

Watch babies for any length of time, and you'll see they are incredibly curious about their world. They don't have an inner critic or any fear, so in a way, they are better off than we are.

A baby takes in an enormous amount of information about themselves and the world around them and interprets it objectively — without the extra filters we have. And they have fun while they learn! We should approach challenges in a similar way.

What if you just gave in to pure curiosity and didn't worry about people judging you for asking "too many questions"? In the past, you may have been discouraged from doing this. However, people asking questions has resulted in so many good things, like inventions, technologies, and healing medicines and procedures. It's the first part of the scientific process. You can learn to work past that inner critic to find your own breakthroughs.

By changing your approach, you can begin to reprogram who you are and what you believe about yourself now — not based only on the messages you received and believed growing up. You get to **choose** what to believe and accept. It's amazing the things you learn about and create in yourself when you build new neural pathways through this process. You can build a new cognitive template for yourself, like a baby, re-raising yourself, ridding yourself of the old template that isn't letting you get to the next ladder rung.

Pick Your Scary Task

You already have your plan, right? What's something you can do that's maybe just a little scary and will help you get to the next ladder rung? Let's make that a new goal.

Here's your task for the Challenge phase:

- What's a step that will challenge you a little?
- When deciding on this challenge, examine your expectations to make sure you aren't setting yourself up to fail because of automatic negative thoughts or not breaking the challenge into manageable pieces.
- If you have a negative/unpleasant belief, look at the opposite or a positive/pleasant belief. This is the belief you want to have in the front of your mind as you go along. Exchange the negative for the positive and practice it. This may seem hard at first, AND you'll get better at it the more you do it.

Now go do that thing! (And celebrate a little bit extra when you do!)

REEVALUATE

Reevaluate goes a step further than Assess in the Healing Investigation chapter. Where the Assess component involves observation and reflection, the Reevaluate component involves looking at the situation and actually using data points to measure things at different stages.

The way you measure your progress can be formal or informal, detailed or simple. The most important thing is to decide what and how you're measuring, how often you're going to measure it (the frequency), and whether you're tracking a specific length of time (duration):

- **Measurement**: You can measure whatever you want. Maybe you decide to track the intensity of specific emotions, such as confidence, hope, or empowerment, on a scale of 1 to 10 every time you check in with yourself.

- **Frequency**: You could decide to track your emotions every day and evaluate the little steps you have achieved. Great! Or perhaps you decide you only have time to track once a week. Also great! Just pick a frequency that helps you stay motivated and isn't too overwhelming.
- **Duration**: Maybe you're measuring how long the step lasted. Was it over a period of minutes, several hours, or even days? For instance, if you measured relief, how long did it last before fading away? If you're measuring sadness, how long did it last before it eased?

Frequency and duration (along with intensity) are also used by medical professionals to track the experience of pain and healing. Pain is what you have been experiencing, and healing is what we are doing.

Look at the Whole Picture

When tracking information, I also remind clients to look beyond each piece of information and include multiple data points. Over time, are they moving on an overall upward trajectory, even if there are dips and plateaus? For instance, the stock market may have a ten-point dip one day, but over the last thirty days, it has ended up twenty points higher than when it began. So, if you're measuring your last thirty days, and you had a bad day yesterday (unpleasant or painful), does that mean nothing is going right? No. It just means there was a *bad* day in the middle of twenty-nine *good* ones.

Two close friends have helped my perspective of unpleasant experiences to be viewed as only that, an experience of a thought, emotion, and body sensation. To take it a step further, consider what it would be like to not categorize an experience as good or bad but instead something we can grow from. Whether you take an action or not, ask yourself what went well. What did not go well? What was the belief you had? Where are you now in the progression of your new belief?

Reevaluation Can Happen in Small Increments

Notice I just said progression? Remember, it's a building **process**. Through Reevaluation, you can form new beliefs that help you **create** (what an empowering word) change.

Here's a personal example. I used to say, "I am not a runner." In late 2020, a close friend said she planned to run a half marathon and wanted me to join her. I lovingly scoffed and dismissed it with a smile.

However, she didn't give up easily. When she broke down the process into bite-sized pieces, I agreed to take the first step. First, she had me do interval running for a mile and evaluate how I felt. As I did this, I was willing to concede that it was probably doable(ish) for me. And I realized I needed to change the way I was speaking to myself because (as I like to say, nerd alert!) my brain was neuroplastic — it was shaping its neural pathways to my beliefs and statements. I had to reevaluate my self-assessment of not being "a runner."

So, I started small. My "all-or-nothing" thinking did not go straight to saying, "I am a runner," which I would not have believed. Instead, I would say, "Sometimes I go running," because that was true. Sticking to the truth and telling that to myself made it easier to accomplish. **Imagine that!** No, literally — imagining it is how it all started! Don't negate the power of your imagination.

Remember when I said to celebrate all wins? I celebrated running a mile, then two, then three. I did it through interval runs. Some people who run a lot would say intervals "aren't really running," but I didn't listen to them. Interval running is essentially **pacing yourself**, and that is so important for life.

When my friend saw I was nearly ready, we signed up for a 5K (3.1 miles). It was in early March 2021, and I was very grateful that several of my family and friends were running with me in the FREEZING temps!

All those accomplishments made me feel more confident and prepared me to run a 10.5K (or 6.5 miles — a quarter marathon!). I was nervous and scared. Thankfully, I was running with two close friends who supported me the whole time.

I eventually ran 15.1K (9.4 miles) with another close friend — the entire loop around White Rock Lake in Dallas.

I signed up to run the BMW Dallas Half Marathon/21.1K in December 2021 with the two friends from the quarter marathon. Even though I had to walk a fair amount of the course due to an injury while training, I completed it —13.1 miles!

I had many thoughts of giving up, but several things kept me going. I wanted to be proud of myself for accomplishing this thing I had never imagined doing. I was so grateful for the family and friends who were there to support me-meeting me at different points along the way with signs, smiles, cheers, and even walking the path (literally and figuratively) with me.

Their Talk component was crucial. We all need someone to cheer us on and/or push us forward at times. When we forget that we are capable, they help us remember.

Evaluate Your Progress

Here are some tasks to help you **notice** your growth and progress:

- Take a regular, periodic "read" of your situation to get data points. This can be as simple as measuring on a scale of 1 to 10 things like your thoughts, beliefs, feelings, emotions, and actions. Maybe it's your mind/body/spirit — whatever categories make sense.
- Track these data points over time so you can see both long-term and short-term progress.
- Find more reasons to celebrate!

UNIFY

Unifying the different aspects of ourselves is key to getting unstuck. When I say different aspects, I mean all of the facets of your being — your emotions, thoughts, physical body, beliefs, values, words, or actions.

A human isn't only a physical body. We're made of vibrational energy. An easy way to think of it is that our bodies are one kind of energy, our thoughts are another, and our emotions are another. All of these energies work together to help us process and move through our life events on multiple, interwoven levels.

I once heard someone say that it's helpful to think of emotions as "e-motions" or "energy in motion." When we are feeling sad or mad, our bodies generate energy that needs to be processed — maybe through tears, intentional breath, or another physical reaction. We even say things like, "I just need to sweat it out" (meaning this is a way the energy of stress can be released), "Just walk it off" (to cool down your temper), or "I need to work off some of this frustration." Emotional energy often creates a physical response to make it easier to notice and then be able to process it through.

Emotions Can Lead to Physical Symptoms and Vice Versa

When you're dealing with a mental or emotional block, like Jordan's fear of driving, you can't just "get rid of it." You can't use a thought to make an emotion go away; it may seem to work for a time, but it will express itself somehow, even subtly.

If not processed or "spent" physically, stress energy will stay in our body. It's like the old video game Pong when the little dot is trapped inside the square and keeps bouncing around against the boundaries. In this case, your body is the square. To keep the energy from being trapped, our bodies do things like make tears and sweat, increase our breathing and heart rate, or even make us physically sick to our stomachs.

When Jordan was terrified of getting back behind the wheel after his accident, he had to work to rewire his neural pathways by experiencing physical safety in a car. Then, he needed to acknowledge it to himself verbally to help his emotions understand that they are seen so that, eventually, they didn't have to keep waving a red warning flag. The accident had occurred in the past. Jordan needed to bring his emotional and physical responses to the present, and his body and words became vehicles for doing that, along with therapeutic tools.

It's important to honor and process emotions. According to many researchers, including Dr. Gabor Maté in his book *When the Body Says No,* we often hold onto negative energy from emotions, beliefs, and thoughts which can lead to physical symptoms. Over time, these symptoms can build and contribute to illness and other somatic issues.[19]

Align Your Words and Beliefs

There's a disconnect when we tell ourselves we value certain things, but we aren't behaving in a way that affirms that — our words and beliefs aren't unified or aligned with our actions, and it makes us feel unsettled.

This is why I couldn't go immediately from "I am not a runner" to "I am a runner." I wouldn't have believed it the moment I said it. Part of me would think, "I'm confused! You just said you weren't a runner. Make up your mind!" I needed to believe what I was saying, so I had to start with a small truth. Small, believable truths also helped Jordan start feeling safe in the car again. He couldn't go from feeling completely unsafe in a car to suddenly believing he was safe. He needed to experience feeling safe in small stages to build on and keep his beliefs unified with his affirmations. (This is a good example of why experiential therapies help heal trauma more than other types of talk therapies.)

Another way to unify and move beliefs forward is to add the word "yet" after a negative statement, leaving it open for change. "I am not a runner" is not the same as "I am not a runner yet." The change is small ~~but~~ AND important. Without the "yet," the belief stays in a limiting form... and, you guessed it, nothing changes if nothing changes. There's no room in the belief for it to change. Like Pong, you've put the square around it, and the little dot is just trapped, trying to get out. If you take away the square by using "yet," the dot isn't trapped in those limits anymore, and the statement becomes truer.

Values are another form of belief, and they can also conflict with each other. Take Fran's situation. She wanted to be there for her kids, but she also needed to keep working late to stay on top of her job. She valued both her family and performing well at her job. Unfortunately, those two values were like different people in different rooms making decisions without talking to each other. Without planning or careful thought, it can be incredibly difficult to balance things that are at odds with one another.

I've had clients do an exercise where they visualize their different values as people and then have conversations with them in their imagination so they can learn why each other's concerns are important. This might feel funny to you at first, and I get it. Still, have you tried it yet? If not (here we go again), nothing changes if nothing changes. (You're going to have that phrase stuck in your head after you finish this book, I'm sure!)

Start Unifying Your Different Facets

Here are some things you can do to ensure the different parts of yourself are aligned and unified to achieve the goal you've been working toward:

- Think about the values you've been writing about. What are your beliefs about them? What limiting beliefs are there? What kinds of small truths can take you forward in some tiny steps? How can you involve your physical body to help build those truths and gain greater confidence? Start practicing those.
- When you practice an affirmation, pay attention to your body. What physical sensations do you notice? Do you feel tension? Release? Where? Do you experience emotions you can identify?
- What happens in your body when you say something untrue? How do you feel mentally, physically, and emotionally?
- Do any of your values seem to get in each other's way? Let's do a visualization exercise and bring them into your mental "room." Ask each of them what's important. Oftentimes, they have the same main goal for you, such as to "be happy" or "be safe," so it's important to ask them how they could work together. Write down what you learn from the conversation and decide if and how to incorporate it into your plan. If the conflicting values can't immediately decide how to work things out or they clash again later, you may need to plan more conversations with them. Make sure to devote the time needed to get your

internal "team" working together — it will be so worth it.[20]

- This process takes practice and consistency. Sometimes, we try something only once and say it didn't work. That's like eating one vegetable and saying you don't feel any healthier or working out twice and complaining that you're not feeling stronger.

Be patient and lean on your support system during your unifying process. They can help you keep on track. If you need additional help, feel free to reach out to me or another coach or therapist who can help you navigate the process.

ALMOST THERE

You have come this far in the book — way to go! I see you!

Remember: You are capable, and your support team is there whenever you need to be reminded of that. Tell them about the challenge you've set for yourself. Ask them to cheer for you. You've got this!

CHAPTER 8

Healing Embodiment

Today is the first day of the rest of your life.

— ABBIE HOFFMAN

The final letter in the TIME acronym is E, for Embodiment. When you finally embody the things that used to be your goals, you've reached a milestone.

This phase is about realizing you've become that next version of you, the one who just does new things as part of her routine without stressing over them. You've moved beyond the Past You and walked into the future as a new, different person. That person doesn't have all the answers, but now she's more comfortable with not having it all figured out. She realizes she's not going to be finished. There will be even more versions of Future Her, and she's excited about that — maybe even looking forward to them.

Using the three components of Healing Embodiment — Live, Give Grace, and Share — we'll talk about how to live with this new Future You.

YOU ARE NOW THE NEXT VERSION OF YOU

What if you achieved the goals you've written in your notebook? What would your next challenge be? How do you feel about that?

I'm not going to sugarcoat it: The Embodiment stage will likely still be uncomfortable as you're practicing it. Yet uncomfortable doesn't mean bad or not perfect, as you've once feared; it's an opportunity to grow.

When you find yourself confronted with your former assumptions and expectations, you'll ~~have to~~ get to (this was a real edit because I am still remembering the power of my words) sort through them and make new decisions that uphold your goals. Honestly, that part never ends because there will always be things in the future that challenge you. Ultimately, these provide an opportunity to make you better and more resilient. They help you to appreciate the good things even more.

LIVE

In Live, you'll do what we were just looking at — you'll make the changes part of your routine by adding incremental steps. You'll actually *live* this next version of you. I absolutely LOVE it when this happens for my clients or anyone!

This was especially true for my client, Fran. Although she liked her boss, he seemed to have conflicting expectations, and, at times, she had a difficult experience with some of their interactions.

At first, she spent a lot of time talking through her feelings about each frustrating situation before even figuring out how to respond. "Am I crazy for feeling frustrated?" she would ask.

"They're your feelings," I would reply. "You're allowed to feel frustrated." She needed validation for her feelings before she could start to change things.

So we started by working on how she could communicate with him about her workload. "Could you tell him how long certain things take?" I asked.

Her eyes lit up. "I could track my time and show him the hours it takes to complete certain tasks," she said. "I would feel much better doing that instead of feeling like I'm just complaining that it takes a long time."

She was astonished by the results from just that small thing. "He had no idea how much time tasks were taking," she told me, "and we're already looking for ways to make things go more quickly."

After achieving that first win, Fran gained the confidence to face other issues. Rather than working through the problem with me beforehand, she would put together a response on her own. She would send it to me and ask, "Does this sound okay?" I'd reply with some feedback, and she'd tweak it and send it.

Soon after, she'd just send me a screenshot of the conversation to share how proud she was of herself and the way she'd managed the situation. Celebrating a "small" win!

Current You Is Now Future You

Months later, as we touched base on things, she said, "I'm still having trouble figuring out how to juggle my homework with the other stuff I have to do in the evenings."

"Wait, what?" I asked, surprised. "Homework from what?"

"Oh! I decided to take an accounting class. It's been a week and a half, and so far, I'm loving it."

"That's great! Are you still working?"

"Oh, yeah — we need the income. I'm just in school part-time in the evenings. I rearranged my work schedule a little to get to one of my early classes."

"Ooh! What did your boss say?"

She smiled. "He's actually been really supportive. I proposed a way I could work around the classes and not miss any time, and he agreed to it."

I was now smiling, too. "Do you realize what you just told me?"

"That I'm a student again!"

I laughed while looking through my notes. "Well, yeah! I'm so happy for you. And it's not just that."

I finally found what I was looking for. "Do you remember three months ago, when you said, 'My boss makes my life crazy, and I don't know how to fix that'? You've fixed that. You have continued to communicate your priorities, and now they have become routine. Plus, you just decided to take classes AND deal with your boss's potential objections — all on your own. That's huge! You didn't even check in with me this time! AND you did it without worrying!"

Her eyes lit up. "You're right!" she said. "I didn't even think about it. I just did it!"

This was definitely a milestone. And it was made up of many individual moments. Fran had worked so hard to get to this point, and her effort had paid off. She was truly living her Future Self and was on to the next part of her journey. Over time, these incremental changes transformed her situation AND her.

GIVE GRACE

The expression "give someone grace" is used a lot in Christian discourse, and yet the richness of this word "grace" can be applied in many non-religious contexts. The definition we'll be using here is "reprieve."

In other words, cut yourself and others some slack. Have patience. Many clients, and I myself, have worked through the belief "I have to be perfect" (and for me, it still comes up, but less so now). Expecting perfection from yourself or others creates a situation that is bound to hamper and disappoint you.

Most of my clients start out as all-or-nothing or black-and-white thinkers. That's a big part of why they're unhappy. They believe they have to get something perfect, or it's wrong or not good enough.

Instead, it's often better to prioritize consistency over perfection. You'll get where you want to be more peacefully, and you might also get there faster.

Perfectionism puts unrealistic boundaries around you. Here's an example: remember when you were a kid, and you pretended the cardboard paper towel tube was a telescope? When you looked through it, you saw what was in the circle and not what was around it — you only saw a small circle of the world.

Perfectionism is like that. You set boundaries so that only what's inside the little circle is acceptable. When you're used to looking through that circle, it's easy to forget there are other things beyond those boundaries. You start believing what's in the circle is the only thing there is. And that's just NOT true.

Removing Unnecessary Boundaries

One of my clients — we'll call her Autumn — grew up in a household with her mom, Terri. Terri was very domineering and had high expectations for Autumn throughout her childhood. And Autumn felt Terri was getting even more demanding as she got older.

Autumn was in her mid-twenties. When she started her career, she decided that in order to save and buy a house, she'd live at home for a while longer. Autumn would save some money, and Terri could use some help with her mortgage and utilities.

It was a good temporary financial arrangement, but Autumn felt like her mom set a lot of unrealistic, stressful expectations for her. There was constant tension in the house, and Terri eventually urged Autumn to go to therapy.

"I don't even know why I'm here," Autumn told me on our first day. "I'm not depressed. My mom wanted me to come here because I'm not happy."

Over time, we realized that part of Autumn's unhappiness was her mother's expectation that she be happy, as if it was a kind of switch she could just turn off and on. Still, Autumn admitted that her mom wasn't wrong about her being unhappy.

"I don't really understand why I'm *not* happy," she confessed. "Or how to be happy."

"Is there anything you feel happy doing?" I asked her.

"I don't know," she said. "Not anything I can think of."

We put this to the side briefly, and as we were talking about something else, she mentioned she'd gotten out her sketchbook for the first time that spring.

"What?! I didn't know you sketch," I said, surprised. "Say more!"

"Oh, well, I don't do it often," Autumn said. "When I start, I just get sucked in, and I don't get anything else done for hours. I can lose a whole day without noticing."

I asked, "Really? So, you feel you have to limit your sketching time?"

"Oh, definitely. I usually only let myself sketch once every couple of months when I have a free day to throw away."

"What if you got to sketch every day?" I asked her.

She shook her head. "Oh, no. That would be dangerous. I'd never get anything else done."

"Not if you set a limit to only sketch a certain amount of time a day," I said. "Maybe start with just ten minutes in the morning while the coffee is brewing? Or some other time when you have a few extra minutes?"

She thought about this. "Hmmm, I suppose that might work."

She started carrying her sketchbook with her and sketching for ten minutes a day during her lunch hour. After a while, she also allowed herself to sketch a little during times when she had nothing else to do, like when she was waiting for her mom at a doctor's appointment. Once, she even sketched when she was stuck in a traffic jam, and the cars didn't move for a half hour.

It took so little time out of each day, but this one activity gave her so much happiness! After a while, she brought in dozens of sketches to show me. She even entered one in a contest at the local art center, and she started taking an advanced drawing class there.

Autumn had been looking at her life through the mental equivalent of that paper towel tube. It was formed of rules she made for herself and those that others had made for her. The world she saw when peering through it was a tiny circle. Nothing she wanted to do fit into that circle.

What she needed to do was expand her vision, which meant gradually cutting off the end of the paper towel tube till it was shorter and shorter. Each time, the circle got bigger. Eventually, she threw out the tube entirely. Her rules and her vision have expanded to see the whole picture.

She just needed to give herself some grace — some slack, some compassion. She eventually also requested this grace from her mother. Once Autumn was able to see the bigger picture and find creative solutions, an entire world opened up to her.

WHEN SLOW IS FAST

We often have unrealistic expectations of ourselves. Our world seems to demand that we do more and more — sometimes to an impossible extent. I love the saying Navy SEALs and firefighters use to explain why this idea of *more* doesn't work. They say, "Slow is smooth; smooth is fast."[21] It seems like it should be the other way around, right? And yet, it totally makes sense.

Think about it: When you rush, rush, rush, you make mistakes, causing more problems for yourself. When you push yourself harder and harder, you get burned out, and you give up. Fast ends up being slow. It creates more problems — mistakes to fix and lost confidence when you feel you've failed. So when we move intentionally, we create a steady pattern to follow that can lead us to flow more freely. How can you change your approach to be more intentional?

What Grace Can You Give Yourself?

What rules have you made that don't need to be there? How is trying to stay in that little paper-towel-tube circle preventing you from exploring other possibilities?

How can you give yourself grace or slack? How can you give others grace by removing narrow expectations from them, too?

SHARE

When you've reached a place where you are living that next version of yourself, it starts to feel natural to want to share more of yourself with others in a way that's different from what you've been used to.

Most of my clients feel overwhelmed in some way prior to working with me. Often, it includes feeling like they are doing so much for others that they don't have time for themselves.

When I talk about the concept of Share, this is not what I mean.

In our definition, Share is sharing parts of your life with others who are open to hearing them and listening. It's not sharing yourself by volunteering for an organization or trying to make a big impression on the whole world. It's sharing little things. This may happen during conversations, even with strangers. A subject comes up that you have some experience with, and you share something you've seen or known that might offer insight. This sort of sharing involves making connections that help others in small ways.

I've been in these kinds of situations while sitting on a plane, just chatting with the person next to me. I don't necessarily do it all the time, and it's not about pushing unwanted advice on others. Sometimes, I'll just offer something like, "I've heard of a way to do that if you're interested — no pressure." If it's something they're open to, great. And if they say they're already working on it in their own way, no problem. It's an invitation, rather than an expectation or judgment, that sends a message that they can learn to trust themselves in life's lessons.

By writing this book, I'm sharing. I worked through the process and got to this version of Future Me; when I look back, I realize that I was living out what I now call TIME. I want you to have the information that helped me, and I believe it can help you.

Sometimes, small things lead to bigger ones. Recently, a former client decided to become a counselor. It's so amazing to see her growth and that she's found her own way of sharing.

It honestly doesn't matter how you choose to Share. No matter what you do, it will make a difference for someone.

Closing the Loop

What Share really does is bring the circle all the way back around. Remember Talk, when you were building your support network and needed people to talk to? They were sharing with you. Now, it's your turn to be part of someone else's support network. Even if you're just listening, you're still sharing your time and empathy with them. The circle is coming back around to help someone else. Healing TIME is a healing circle.

It doesn't have to be a grand gesture. It could be as simple as sharing an article with someone on social media or sharing an experience you had that can help someone feel recognized and validated — letting them know they're not the only one in their situation or they're not the only one who cares.

Sharing can just mean being aware when someone may need a moment of your time and attention. It becomes organic; it feels more natural, whereas before, it probably didn't. The difference is that you're coming from a confident, empowered place instead of feeling obligation — like you *should* help someone or do something. Now, you see it as opportunities around you.

EMBODIMENT MINDSET

What does Embodiment look like for you? Think about what it would be like if these current challenges you're facing were over. What would you do? What would the next goal be? What would your life look like? How would you feel? When the depression, health issues, anxiety, or whatever else is holding you back lifts, what will it feel like?

Write the answers down as if Future You were seeing them in her present moment. "I am happy. I have a life I want, and my health is great. I'm confident and empowered. I can [insert your challenge here] without even thinking about it. Because of all of these things, I'm now going to [insert new goal here]. I know I can do it."

Do some fears and disbelief still come up as you are writing this from the eyes of your Future Self? If so, make a new page in your notebook for them. Then, look at them through an Embodiment lens. What can you do to embody your new future and dispel these negative emotions and beliefs? What small, incremental steps could you take to achieve the future-self state you've written about? Write those down, too. Start creating a plan for doing some of them. Think of Autumn's sketching. Even one small step can make a significant difference!

FILLING YOUR CUP

You may notice when you reach Embodiment that you have more to give than you previously did. Even if you feel your tank isn't quite full, your new way of doing things can get you there.

I've had times when I'm in a great mood, but a friend has had the opposite and may hesitate to share. Amazingly, where this once might have been draining, it can now sometimes refill my cup and I'm able to be a support.

Of course, there are days when I feel very tired and others when I am feeling neutral. In all of these, I am more connected to my body in a healthy way to assess my emotional and social battery. Just like my cell phone needs to rest and recharge, I still need to listen to my body to do the same.

Now, my entire mindset is different. I've learned to say things differently to myself, and I want to show you how as well. I have included three favorites here.

Tip #1: "I Get To" vs. "I Have To"

Here's a mindset exercise I love. Think of something you don't like to do but AND have to do anyway. "I have to pay the bills." Hardly anyone likes doing that, and we don't have much of a choice.

Now, what if you said it differently? "I get to pay the bills."

Suddenly, it's something you're grateful for. And really, isn't it great that you can pay the bills? Paying the bills for your residence means you have shelter. Your energy bills mean your shelter is heated and cooled in all weather. Your internet bill means you have a connection for communication, entertainment, and work. These are things to be grateful for.

This method works for many things. "I have to go to this work function," turns into, "I get to go to this work function." Fill in the blank. Suddenly, obligations become opportunities. Don't worry; you can still have boundaries to care for yourself.

Tip #2: Choose Gratitude to Thrive

Did you know gratitude can improve your physical health? There's a study that shows how gratitude positively affects your physiology. According to Heartmath, focusing on appreciative feelings can smooth your heart rhythm and provide cardiovascular benefits for your body.[22]

Conversely, anger and frustration can create strain on the heart and eventually lead to some serious health issues. Based on this information, practicing gratitude during the day — especially during times of stress — can have huge health benefits. Your mind is a powerful tool for transforming your life in many ways, including helping to preserve your body's physical health.

I'm not saying you should suppress anger or other negative emotions, though — doing that is unhealthy. It's important to let ourselves acknowledge, validate, and experience emotions, particularly when we create a safe enough environment to do so. That allows us to release the energy of the emotion and get unstuck.

When you do that, you will find that you can actually be grateful for the frustrating or negative-feeling experience later. It has not only helped you grow, but has also led to other things that helped you grow. You can leave behind the all-or-nothing idea that pain is only and always *bad*. When you get to this point, you will know you've made it through a cycle of change.

Tip #3: Unwrap the Gift of Life

The unknown doesn't have to be frightening. Some of the best gifts are surprises. When you unwrap your gifts, you don't know what's inside. Why can't the unknown in life bring you delight just as easily? You wouldn't turn down a birthday gift because you don't know what's inside the box, right? Why would you do that with your future? Why not embrace the surprises?

CONFRONT YOUR SUCCESS EXERCISE

What are some potential negatives to getting what you want? How can you think about these differently?

Part 1: List the potential downsides of achieving the goal(s) you've been working on in this book. Use your imagination.

For instance, Fran told me that one downside of being able to successfully deal with her boss's conflicting expectations might be that she'd come off to him as too complaining. She'd get what she wanted at the cost of ruining their relationship.

When Autumn was navigating ways to be happy, it seemed that she was afraid that doing what made her happy (drawing) would keep her from being focused on her career. It was almost as if happiness was a distraction. She could get what she wanted in one thing, but it would ruin another thing.

Marie felt if she pursued her own health solutions, others would see her as foolish for listening to "unapproved" authorities. She worried that she might find health solutions but at the expense of others' respect.

These concerns were part of the reason they weren't able to move forward.

For me, writing this book meant I ~~have to~~ **get to** be vulnerable and open. Being vulnerable and open can feel scary. I am putting myself out there for others to possibly judge. This was a downside that made me hesitate. We all have these potential costs of success. Knowing them is the first step to getting through them.

Part 2: Now, reframe those potential downsides as positive or pleasant outcomes.

Fran realized that being more assertive didn't mean she'd have to be disrespectful to her boss. She could communicate and work with him to find solutions rather than judge herself by saying she was complaining.

Autumn decided to see happiness as a way of balancing her life as well as something that could possibly enhance her career. It didn't have to be either/or. It was just another part of her life.

Marie decided that if she was able to find her own health solutions, it meant she was actually wise, and her wisdom would get her far. She has since inspired others to take charge of their own health.

I chose to write this book because, like you, I've experienced painful emotions and beliefs not living out my values, and I've learned how to do the work needed to heal. Putting myself out there in a book can feel scary because I can't control what other people think, AND that helps me believe that *what I can change* is how I feel about it. Through my choosing this vulnerability, many people may be helped by reading this, and I also know the things I learn from this experience will help me grow as a person.

How can you reframe the story of your own outcome?

CHAPTER 9

Are You Worth the Time?

The best use of life is love. The best expression of love is time. The best time to love is now.

— RICK WARREN

We've looked at many different stories throughout this book, including mine. In each one, the biggest question the person had to answer for themselves was how they were currently viewing and experiencing their relationship with Time and how they could utilize it differently to make a needed change.

This isn't a question of efficiency, prioritization, or multitasking. It is a question of *value*. They'd been spending their time on thoughts, behaviors, and even people that didn't reflect their values, particularly all the different, important parts of themselves. This disconnect between their values and their choices showed in the way they felt about themselves and affected their mental and emotional well-being. If you aren't making progress, what is the reason?

MARIE'S TRANSFORMATION

I love to tell Marie's story because it started with her not believing she could find healing — she felt she was wasting her time.

She realized she'd been unintentionally devaluing herself simply by how she viewed her time. "I thought time was either something I didn't have or maybe didn't deserve to spend on myself," she said. "I didn't believe at first that slowing down, trying again, and taking time to devote to self-care could work. I had tried many times before, and nothing ever changed."

And the worst part for Marie was that through those early struggles, she felt she was totally alone.

What she had really been fighting was a false idea — that she was wasting time on things she believed couldn't happen. With that thinking, she couldn't really allow herself to truly heal.

When she shifted to seeing Time as giving her *opportunities to heal*, everything changed. For that to happen, she had to understand that her goals weren't selfish or unreasonable. Marie said, "There is a saying that goes something like, 'Self-care is not selfish: You can't pour from an empty cup.' I see that now. How can I be a caregiver for my parents if I can't take care of myself?"

With encouragement from her support network, she continued her success by finding a functional medicine doctor, building healthier daily habits, focusing on small wins rather than her previous all-or-nothing mindset, and making her health and wellness a priority.

Now, almost a year later, she can look back and see the two major reasons for her success. "I didn't give up, and I afforded myself time... time to fill my empty cup, time to find what would work for me, and time to heal," she said.

Invest in Your Future Self

Valuing yourself is an expression of love. If you don't love yourself, you won't give yourself what you need, and you can't give others what they need. Aren't you worth the time it will take to find healing? Declare that. Protect that value. If you don't, who will?

Think about it this way. Do you want to have what you say you really want — better health, less anxiety, more freedom, etc.? If so, what thoughts and behaviors can you invest in that will get that result for you, and which will not? Which thoughts show you value yourself, and which don't? Which behaviors are worth doing, and which are not? Which people value and support your growth, and which do not?

I realize you can't make everything that doesn't help you just go away. And there are always going to be people who don't support or value you. The point is that these people shouldn't be the major influences in your life. They should not be able to affect how you view yourself. You don't need to accept what they tell you or what they expect of you without evaluating it for yourself.

Remember: You can allow yourself to view Time as your ally or your enemy when deciding whether to invest in your future self. With Time as an extension of your higher power and you as a co-creator, you have the free will to work with Time in productive or unproductive ways. Remember how I described fear as False Evidence Appearing Real? If your mindset is in a place of fear, it will limit your ability to use Time's power productively because you won't feel open to possibilities that could take you to better places. When you make Time your ally, you can reclaim your power.

WHAT ARE YOU SAYING YES OR NO TO?

Have you heard the saying, "The only thing that gets in the way of a great thing is a good thing."? I don't remember where I heard it, but it's often true.

What's the "good enough" thing you're settling for that's keeping you from doing the great thing you really want to do? Hmmm... that's an interesting thought, isn't it?

There's another piece of wisdom I like that says, "When you say yes to one thing, you are saying no to something else."

This is HUGE! Think about everything you do each day. Each thing you do, you are choosing over something else.

When you choose to keep thinking something is impossible, you are saying no to thinking it's possible. When you choose to do the same thing you've been doing, you are saying no to a change that could lead to new opportunities. As cheesy as it may sound, the only difference between "I'm Possible" and "Impossible" is a space and apostrophe. It's really not a big difference at all.

Sometimes, it can be that simple.

If you think about it that way, shouldn't you be discerning about what you say yes to? When you say yes to getting back into your comfy yet confining cocoon, you're saying no to learning how to fly. When you say yes to doing the same things you've always done and feel terrible, you are saying no to doing something that will put you on a new path — a path to feeling better.

WOW!

It can't get any plainer than that.

As with planting a tree, the best time to have made that change is years ago — AND the next best time is today.

The Cost Is Greater Than You Think

Think of the things in your life that frustrate you. What are they costing you in terms of those categories in Chapter 1, such as mental health, physical well-being, relationships, and opportunities?

Think about it — with every no, you've been refusing a future you could have, although you haven't seen it yet. It may seem hard to think of that as a loss. How can you lose something you've never had?

And yet, there's a term for it: opportunity cost. This is the unknown cost of making one choice over another when the unchosen alternative may lead to a greater return.[23]

So, what if you start turning yes and no around? What if you start saying no to the things that aren't helping you and yes to the things that are? What might you gain?

Sure, there are no guarantees. I can't say to you, "If you just do these things, you'll magically get a bunch of new opportunities, and your whole life will turn around." That isn't true. There's no assurance that a choice will make the difference you want.

However, you already know that what you're currently doing isn't working. And, based on past evidence, that's not likely to change. After all, how many years have you been testing it? How many more do you need before you decide it's not a productive strategy? There's a reason for the saying, "The definition of insanity is doing the same thing over and over and expecting a different result." Einstein is credited with saying, "We cannot solve our problems with the same thinking we used when we created them." I couldn't find a source for those exact words, but whether or not he said them, they're a good way to look at things.

Remember: Small, incremental steps add up over time. Investing a few minutes in yourself is like putting a nickel into a piggy bank. Sure, it's only five cents. And yet, over time, you can end up with a couple hundred dollars. That couple hundred dollars allows you to invest in something larger than what the nickel would have, and you can make even more on that investment.

The *self* you have now has a lot more skill, confidence, and understanding than the one you started out with. Thus, by investing those nickels in yourself, you're putting resources into your own bank. That means when opportunities come along, you'll have the capacity to make the most of them.

Over time, the cost of not investing in yourself is astronomical. I've been there. I know what it's like to pay that price. And I also know that it's possible to escape that trap.

You can choose how to **align** with Time and your values. I know you can do it. And I know that if you decide to, you will.

What Lessons Are We Saying Yes or No To?

We can choose what to learn, and unfortunately, we can choose lessons that won't take us forward over those that will. Fran almost fell into this trap by choosing to focus on her anger about her job situation over ways to move forward.

"It seems like there's something you need to learn from this," I said. "You've learned to honor your emotions, and that's great. However, you seem stuck in your anger."

"I feel angry because the expectations are impossible."

"All right. What is the reason impossible expectations cause you to feel angry?"

"Because they're not fair."

"What is the reason that causes you to feel angry?"

She paused, surprised. "Well ... I guess because there's no way to achieve them. I feel hopeless. There's no way I can't fail." Her brow furrowed. "My boss must just not care about me at all."

"Let's look at things differently. If you don't change anything you're doing, the situation is destined to fail because of the unreasonable expectations being placed on you," I said. "So why not give yourself the opportunity to succeed instead? Why not talk to your boss about the expectations?"

Fran could suddenly see something she originally couldn't. She grinned at me. "Well, why not?" We both laughed.

Fran could have chosen to teach herself the lesson that her chaotic situation was her boss's fault. Yet that lesson was about him having all the power — a hopeless-feeling lesson that would just keep her stuck, feeling like a victim, and still angry.

Instead, she chose to start defining her boundaries and taking responsibility for her own success instead of blaming her boss. It became a learning opportunity. How could she learn to work with him and do a good job while also not being overwhelmed? She had been treating the relationship as if she was just an order-taker, and he was the order-giver. Now, however, she was now starting to see it instead as a collaboration with an end goal.

She had to recognize her own power so she could see how and where to shift this dynamic.

Remember the illustration with the spiral? That's what a growing, evolving person looks like.

That kind of growth comes from learning the lessons that teach us to grow instead of learning the lessons that teach us to stay safe or feel vindicated or give us reasons to focus on anything but our own actions.

Think about a current situation you're frustrated with. It could be a frustration about what someone else is doing or a situation in general.

Are you learning, or are you just getting mad or frustrated? What are you teaching yourself? What else could you learn that is more productive instead of it being someone else's fault, and you're at their mercy?

The funny thing was, as we've already seen, Fran's boss had no idea he was setting such conflicting expectations for her (and, it turns out, for others, too!). He didn't fully know what their jobs involved on a day-to-day basis. And here, Fran had no idea that he had no idea. She hadn't yet given herself the opportunity to find out by talking to him about things!

When she finally told him some of what she'd been going through, he was mortified and glad she told him.

They eventually had a good laugh over it, and Fran learned a valuable lesson: Don't leap to conclusions about anyone's motives or knowledge.

When you say yes to the right lesson, you have no idea what good can result. The cost of not doing so remains hidden, and yet we trust that it was the best decision. The worst thing is that you may never realize you're paying that cost.

BE THE BUTTERFLY

During the change process, making progress isn't always predictable. We can still fall into old habits where old assumptions and ideas try to take hold. We need to stay mindful of that and continue practicing new habits to keep our momentum moving forward.

This reminds me of what a caterpillar must feel like after it changes into a butterfly. It's an odd transition. One minute, you're crawling along, happily munching leaves, and the next, you feel the need to build this thing called a cocoon. When you come out, you and your relationship to the world are totally different. You now have these awkward wings, and you can apparently fly, if only you knew how. It's a challenge because there's this crazy wind blowing you around. And you can no longer hide in the foliage like you once did. You're too bright and showy for that. It's a much more chaotic place than the peaceful little branches you used to hang out on. Those were the days, right?!

Faced with these new challenges, you might seriously think about getting back into that cocoon. It was so much safer. But you realize that now, with your wings, you don't fit. You can't go back.

So, you have two choices: You can spend your time as a butterfly wishing you were still a caterpillar, or you can spend your time learning to enjoy all that being a butterfly has to offer. Which would you rather do?

Sorry (mostly) to be cliché again, but be like the butterfly. Spread your wings and learn to fly! It will get easier the more you practice, and there's a whole new world out there for you to explore.

YOU HAVE THE POWER

So, here we are. The cocoon is just the butterfly's line in the sand.

You can use your time however you want. That's within your power or control. When you continued to feel powerless, it wasn't because you didn't have any power. It was because you hadn't accepted that you are the one who chooses how to use what Time offers.

Past You was using it to tell yourself that certain things were impossible, unrealistic, or bad, and not using it to question whether those statements were even true. You'd been trying to get back in the cocoon instead of testing and strengthening your wings. Old habits die hard.

Remember when I told myself I couldn't start my own practice and applied for different school counselor positions instead? I had made so much progress, and yet I tried to go back into my cocoon. And darn it! I didn't fit there anymore. It was too small. So here I am now, so grateful I didn't fit!

Somewhere in my mind, I was already testing my wings. I was thinking differently. I didn't *have to* make that big change; I *got to* make it. I allowed myself to **dream** and make the change I really wanted.

By reading this book, you've already begun to test your wings. If you keep going, you can discover what's really possible.

CHAPTER 10

How to Get Started

*All the flowers of all the tomorrows
are planted in the seeds of today.*
— NATIVE AMERICAN PROVERB

In one of my favorite movies, *Passengers,* a huge interstellar spaceship built on Earth is heading to colonize a distant planet. Spoiler alert — this section details a lot of what this movie is about, so if you think you want to watch it, you can skip to the next section!

All the people on the ship are in suspended animation pods for most of the journey. Without the pods, they would age and die before they reached the colony. The ship is fully automated, and everyone is supposed to wake up at a certain time to prepare for landing on the planet.[24]

Unfortunately, one of the passengers' pods malfunctions, and he wakes up long before he's supposed to. Since he's the only person awake, he's lonely and depressed. He can't figure out how to make his pod take him back in. (It kind of sounds like the butterfly not being able to go back into the cocoon!)

Being awakened turns out to be a good thing, though, because eventually, he learns that the ship is not on course to make it to the colony. Without action, everyone aboard will die. I won't tell you everything that happens next, but while he and two others are able to save the rest of the crew from death, they all end up spending the rest of their lives on the ship instead of at their planned destination.

There's a lesson in the story. At first, the situation seemed terrible — a horrible sacrifice they didn't want to make. Then, somewhere along the way, they realized it was also an opportunity. Not only were they able to save their shipmates, but they also forged strong relationships, learned how to do things they'd never known how to do, and gave their fellow travelers the chance to wake up and live.

This is obviously an extreme situation, and none of us is likely to find ourselves in one that's anything like it (thankfully!). And yet, it does describe how we can view Time as either an ally or an enemy.

All the passengers on the ship had decided to do something totally new in leaving the current familiar to go to the unknown future. They drew their line in the sand — between Earth and another planet. They faced an entirely unforeseen set of circumstances, and each would play a role in the new situation — likely in ways they couldn't even foresee. They left their Past Selves behind and embarked on a journey, putting their faith in their Future Selves and destiny.

This is the way Time works. It works for us as we experience each present moment. This book isn't meant to teach you a way to be selfish and only look out for yourself. It's meant to show you a better way to align with Time so you can achieve the goals you identified when we began and identify opportunities you can create in your now to help you get to Future You.

Healing TIME Recap

We've covered a lot of ground as we've gone through the different steps of this journey. I think a brief review of the Healing TIME elements might be helpful before you move forward to experience what's on the other side of your line in the sand.

Talk: Remember to find and grow a support network. You don't have to have dozens of people in it — it's about quality, not quantity. Who do you admire, look up to, or want to be more like? Who will be in your corner and cheer you on? Who won't let you give up? These are your people. Stay away from people who are negative or apathetic. Unfortunately, they're not able to be there for you.

Investigation: Start looking at what you're telling yourself and what others have told you. Begin to investigate your false assumptions and limiting beliefs. And also, start looking for the new things on the other side of your line in the sand — the new beliefs and goals you are setting for yourself. You get to choose those things. Become your own detective. Learn who you really are — not who you feel you should be because of what you've read or what people have told you — and choose accordingly.

Movement: Start taking action, however small it seems. You don't have to do giant things to achieve your goals. Trying to do that can be overwhelming and disappointing. You're human, with a lot of stuff going on in your life, so don't try to do it all at once. Remember: Consistency over perfection applies here.

Embodiment: At first, you may not even notice the subtle changes when you start to become the next version of You. Ask your support network to pay attention and help you recognize when you begin to embody the goals you set out to reach. Most importantly, ask them to celebrate this milestone with you. My prediction and wish for you is that it is the first of many!

When should you start practicing these things? You know what I'm going to say — the best time was twenty years ago, AND the second best time is NOW. Today! This moment!

WHAT'S YOUR BEST POSSIBLE FUTURE?

I hope that while reading this book, you've been doing the exercises and practicing what you've been learning. If not, it's never too late to go back and do so.

There are many people who believe it's possible to create a version of Heaven on Earth. What do you think? Do you dare to dream that big? What if we all did? What could our world be?

Think about it this way. What is Heaven? A portion of it is peace, rest, perfect love, and eternal joy. Is it possible to have some reflection of that in our present lives? I think it is.

H.G. Wells said, "We must not allow the clock and the calendar to blind us to the fact that each moment of life is a miracle and mystery." He was talking about not letting Chronos (measured linear time) overwhelm us, which could cause us to forget the lesson of Kairos (opportunity, perspective) — that every moment holds new possibilities. If we don't keep looking for those, we will miss them.

Remember that it only takes one small step to get started on the path to Future You. So many things you want to do are possible. You now have many tools to help you partner with Time and achieve what you envisioned. All you need to do is put those tools into action. You may not save a ship full of fellow passengers, yet you may have an impact you can't even imagine.

I'm Rooting for You

Some languages have words for things English doesn't. One of these is a term I enjoy: *firgun*. It's a Hebrew word that means "to root for someone, to be supportive, not to rain on someone else's parade."[25] I want to cheer you on!

With that in mind, I'd love to hear if this book has helped you in even a small way. Send me an email and tell me how. Just think of me as playing a small role in your support network (that's true whether you reach out to me or not!).

I wish you the VERY best as you start on this journey to find out who you are on the other side of your line in the sand. Just know (and imagine) that I'm cheering for you every step of the way.

WOULD YOU SPARE A QUICK MOMENT?

Remember that Share facet we talked about? Here's your chance to do something small yet significant.

If you have found this book valuable, would you please take a moment right now and leave an honest review? There are other people who might benefit from the book, and your review will help them find it. You'll be paying it forward. Small gestures can make a big impact.

Thank you so much — from me and Future Readers who appreciate your help. ☺

Sincerely,
Rebecca

Endnotes

1   Brené Brown, "Own Our History. Change the Story," October 10, 2023, https://brenebrown.com/articles/2015/06/18/own-our-history-change-the-story/.

2   "Unleash the Potential of Your Reticular Activating System," Trauma Research UK, August 18, 2023, https://traumaresearchuk.org/blog/unleash-the-potential-of-your-reticular-activating-system/.

3   UNICEF, "The Formative Early Years of a Child's Life Demand a Nurturing Environment and Attentive Care," accessed April 14, 2025, https://data.unicef.org/topic/early-childhood-development/overview/.

4   CDC, "About Adverse Childhood Experiences," October 8, 2024, https://www.cdc.gov/aces/about/index.html.

5   Peter Grinspoon, "How to Recognize and Tame Your Cognitive Distortions," Harvard Health Publishing, May 4, 2022, https://www.health.harvard.edu/blog/how-to-recognize-and-tame-your-cognitive-distortions-202205042738.

6   Guest contributor, "The Ancient Greeks Had Two Words for Time: Chronos and Kairos – the Difference?" *Greek City Times*, August 14,

2022, https://greekcitytimes.com/2022/08/14/
ancient-greeks-two-word-time.

7   Cynthia Lee, "The Stranger Within: Connecting
    with our Future Selves," UCLA Newsroom, April 9,
    2015, https://newsroom.ucla.edu/stories/the-strang-
    er-within-connecting-with-our-future-selves.

8   Mel Robbins (@melrobbins), X (formerly Twitter)
    post, September 18, 2021, https://x.com/melrobbins/
    status/1439352284123643908?lang=en.

9   Nahrain Raihan and Mark Cogburn, *Stages of
    Change Theory*, StatPearls Publishing, January
    2025, https://www.ncbi.nlm.nih.gov/books/
    NBK556005/.

10 Andrea Liebross, "Why You're Resisting Delegation
    in Your Business and What You Can Do About
    It," *She Thinks Big (p*odcast), April 12, 2024,
    https://podcasts.apple.com/us/podcast/why-
    youre-resisting-delegation-in-your-business-and/
    id1543392747?i=1000676617625.

11 Ed Rush, *God Talks: How to Have a Friendship with
    God (Even If You've Made a Million Mistakes)* (God
    Talks Inc., 2023), 51.

12 H. J. Klein, R. B. Lount, Jr, H. M. Park, and B. J.
    Linford, "When goals are known: The effects of au-
    dience relative status on goal commitment and per-
    formance," *Journal of Applied Psychology* 105, no. 4
    (2020): 372–389. https://doi.org/10.1037/apl0000441.

13 Kristin D. Neff, "Self-Compassion: Theory,
    Method, Research, and Intervention," *Annual
    Review of Psychology* 74, (2023):193–218. https://doi.
    org/10.1146/annurev-psych-032420-031047.

14 The Honey Badger Project, https://wearehoneybad-
    gers.com/.

15 Carolyn C. Ross, "How to Create New Core Beliefs," *Psychology Today*, January 23, 2022, https://www. psychologytoday.com/us/blog/real-healing/202201/ how-to-create-new-core-beliefs.

16 Amen Clinics, "Negative Thinking: Do You Have an ANT Infestation in Your Head?" August 5, 2024, https://www.amenclinics.com/blog/nega- tive-thinking-do-you-have-an-ant-infestation-in- your-head/.

17 Tara Brach, "Transcript: The Sacred Pause," October 14, 2018, https://www.tarabrach.com/ transcript-sacred-pause/.

18 Brendon Burchard, Instagram post, November 18, 2024, https://www.instagram.com/reel/DCheIZFJve N/?igsh=enptbnA0OG43bGgx.

19 Gabor Maté, MD., *When the Body Says No: Exploring the Stress-Disease Connection* (Trade Paper Press, 2011).

20 Exercise loosely based on the Internal Family Systems Therapy by Richard Schwartz, *Psychology Today*, https://www.psychologytoday.com/us/ therapy-types/internal-family-systems-therapy.

21 Navy Seal.com, "Slow Is Smooth, Smooth Is Fast: Navy Seals' Efficiency Secret," October 2, 2023, https://www.navyseal.com/ slow-is-smooth-smooth-is-fast/

22 HeartMath, "An Appreciative Heart Is Good Medicine," July 2, 2009, https://www.heartmath. org/articles-of-the-heart/personal-development/ an-appreciative-heart-is-good-medicine/

23 *Merriam-Webster*, s.v. "opportunity cost" (n), ac- cessed April 15, 2025, https://www.merriam-web- ster.com/dictionary/opportunity%20cost.

24 Morten Tyldum, dir. *Passengers.* 2016; Sony Pictures
    Entertainment.

25 Gila Brand, "Firgun: An Optimistic
    Little Word," Made in Jerusalem, June
    22,2014, https://blog.madeinjlm.org/
    firgun-an-optimistic-little-word-42e862233e0c.

About the Author

Rebecca Hogg, MA, LPC, is the founder and owner of Canvas Counseling & Wellness, PLLC. What do a playground physics investigation on inflation, a failed school skipping attempt, and skydiving have in common? These are just a few of the defining adventures in the early life of Rebecca. From the day she was born, she was craning her neck to see the world around her, and she hasn't stopped wanting to know more about the human experience and sharing it with others in meaningful and fun ways. Sometimes, her curiosity has worked out, and sometimes, it's gotten her into trouble. Nevertheless, it has remained a constant in her life, challenging her to try new things in spite of fear.

Rebecca appreciates the value of lessons learned and the beauty in the simple explorations and interconnectedness of life, our world, and the universe.

She has also realized along the way that she's very often drawn to the concept of t/Time in movies, music, and TV, and she sees it as an integral presence in her understanding of life. In *Healing TIME*, she draws from both her life experiences and her work as a counselor to offer others the tools to develop new ways of thinking that will change their relationship with Time so they can become who they're meant to be.

To support others in their healing time, Rebecca offers customized therapy intensives and personalized therapeutic coaching programs. Her holistic therapy modalities address a variety of issues, including trauma and mind-body connection/somatic concerns. Rebecca developed her therapeutic coaching program for those who don't have time for therapy or don't feel therapy would work for them, yet they need emotional support through a stressful time or through chronic health and pain. In addition to her therapy and therapeutic coaching services, she is also available for consulting, podcast appearances, and speaking engagements. She continues to write as she learns and grows so be ready for more books and/or resources!

CONNECT WITH REBECCA

E-mail: healingtime@canvascw.com

YouTube: @CanvasCounselingWellness

Website: CanvasCW.com

Facebook: @rebeccadhogg

Instagram: @rebeccadhogg

LinkedIn: @rebeccadhogg

Acknowledgements

God gave you a gift of 86,400 seconds today.
Have you used one to say "thank you"?
— WILLIAM ARTHUR WARD

I can't end the book without thanking all of the individuals — family, friends, mentors, colleagues, clients, and numerous bystanders — whom I have met throughout the years. Thanks to you, I had the opportunity to heal, grow, and find the treasures hidden in the moments of life.

I also especially want to thank those who listened to me when I needed reassurance — especially when I felt I was all over the place! Your validation and support meant — and still mean — more than you realize.

I would not be where I am without any of you. Thank you so much for being part of my journey. If it is meant to be, I look forward to our paths crossing.

For More Resources...

As a small "Thank You" for purchasing my book, I'd like to give you some additional tools for *Healing TIME!*

YOU'LL RECEIVE:

- **VALUES CLARIFICATION** worksheet
- "If Time Were a Person..." **JOURNAL PROMPTS**
- Common **CORE BELIEFS** (see if yours are on it!)
- **SOMATIC EMBODIMENT PRACTICES**
- And **MORE!**

THEY'RE ALL AVAILABLE HERE!

https://canvascw.com/book/downloads

Are You Tired of Doing This All Alone?

{ Sometimes, working with a COACH and/or THERAPIST can help you kickstart the FUTURE YOU much faster than trying to do it ALL BY YOURSELF. }

If you need more help to overhaul the overwhelm and get to a place of increased clarity, self-trust, and internal peace, feel free to reach out! I would be honored to be part of your Talk support network.

Together, we'll create a **customized plan** to start transforming your life in a way that honors the next version of you — even if you're not sure who that is yet.

TO LEARN MORE ABOUT PRICING AND SET UP A CONSULT CALL, VISIT:

https://www.canvascw.com/
therapeutic-coaching

www.ingramcontent.com/pod-product-compliance
Lightning Source LLC
Chambersburg PA
CBHW061758120626
46550CB00005B/2049